On the Economic Theory of Socialism
Oskar Lange has lectured at the University
of Cracow, the University of California,
and the University of Chicago, and is the
author of books in Polish, German, and English
on problems of economic theory. He is
now Professor of Economics at the
University of Warsaw.
Fred M. Taylor, a distinguished American
economist, was professor at the University of
Michigan from 1904 until his death in 1932,
and the author of PRINCIPLES OF
ECONOMICS and other volumes. The paper
reprinted here was his presidential address
to the American Economic Association.
Benjamin E. Lippincott is professor
of political science at the University of
Minnesota, and author of VICTORIAN
CRITICS OF DEMOCRACY.

University of Minnesota Press

On the Economic Theory of Socialism

Oskar Lange
Fred M. Taylor

edited by Benjamin E. Lippincott

McGraw-Hill Book Company
New York Toronto London

Third printing 1952
Fourth printing 1956

First McGraw-Hill Paperback Edition, 1964

PRINTED IN THE UNITED STATES OF AMERICA

PREFACE

THIS volume is the second in a series on the problem of government control of the economic order. In the first volume of the series it was pointed out that the political scientist cannot hope to deal intelligently with the problem of control—and it is his problem ultimately—unless he first acquaints himself with the nature of what is to be controlled. The political scientist is interested in two main types of control: control of a capitalist and control of a socialist economy. This volume is concerned with the latter. A later volume will deal with the former.

We have included in this volume papers by Fred M. Taylor and Oskar Lange. These economists have dealt with a socialist economy on the ground of economic theory and its possibility in practice. Preceding these essays is an introduction of some length. Its purpose is not only to provide something of a background for the technical economic essays, but also to sketch the main argument of the essays for the reader who is not a specialist in economics. The introduction has a further purpose: to point out briefly the significance of the economic essays for the problem of government control of the economic order.

I wish to thank the editors of the *American Economic Review* and the *Review of Economic Studies* for their kind permission to reprint papers from their journals.

BENJAMIN E. LIPPINCOTT

University of Minnesota
February, 1938

CONTENTS

INTRODUCTION

Benjamin E. Lippincott

INTRODUCTION

By BENJAMIN E. LIPPINCOTT

I

IN the folklore of capitalism is the belief that a socialist economy is impracticable. Like many other beliefs in capitalist culture, this is widely held not only by the man in the street, but also by the economist. Of all the objections that have been raised against socialism, none have been more telling than this: that socialism cannot be worked out in practice. Men of good will might agree that a socialist state of the democratic type is superior to a capitalist on social and moral grounds, but they have given little consideration to such a state, for they have assumed that it is impracticable. If they were asked to explain their position, they would probably say two things: that socialism would not provide adequate incentives to spur men to effort, enterprise, and invention; that socialism would not be feasible economically.

None have been more responsible for the currency of this belief than the socialists themselves. Not that Marxian economists have been unaware of the problem, but they have thought about it in terms of an inadequate concept of Ricardian economics.[1] Marxian economists since Marx

[1] See below, pages 132 and 141. Cf. Oskar Lange, "Marxian Economics and Modern Economic Theory," *Review of Economic Studies,* June, 1935.

have generally been dominated by the labor theory of value, with the result that they have found little or no significance in the economic tools developed by orthodox economics. Yet the irony is, as the following essays will show, that they have neglected the very thought that could have led them to an impressive technical demonstration that socialism is practicable on economic grounds.

If Marxian economists are largely responsible for failing to show how the everyday economics of socialism might be worked out in practice, socialist writers other than economists must share some of the responsibility. Writers on history, sociology, and political science like the Webbs, Tawney, and Laski have done admirable work in constructing institutions for a socialist state, but they have not pressed for an inquiry into the economics of such a state, even though the economics might vitally affect what they have constructed. They have not sufficiently considered the economic conditions that must be satisfied if a socialist state is to equal or to improve upon the standard of life provided by capitalism. Nor have they given adequate attention, from the technical point of view, to the economic advantages and disadvantages of socialism as compared with capitalism. Yet unless they have some understanding of the economics of a socialist state, and unless they are able to present its case on economic grounds, even though they are historians and political scientists, they can hardly hope to persuade the mass of men to believe in the state which they advocate.

Writers like the Webbs, Tawney, and Laski have shown little interest in the technical economic problems of a socialist state because they have considered these problems to be outside their special fields of study, and because they have held that the question of the desirability of socialism is not essentially an economic question. In addition, they have been impressed with the shortcomings of the chief doctrines of Marxian economics—the labor theory of value and the doctrine of surplus value—and have generally found that orthodox economists were uninterested in or hostile to the consideration of a socialist state.

Almost all socialists have been influenced in some degree by the Marxian view that the problem of the actual working of a socialist economy could not be tackled until the socialists themselves had obtained control of the state. Socialists, in other words, have approached their problem to no small extent from the historical point of view, and as a result have held that very little could be said about the future until men had actually arrived there. Many socialists, furthermore, have drawn a certain fatalism from Marx's dialectical view of history; assuming that socialism is inevitable, they have thought that the problem of a socialist economy would in the nature of things work itself out. Other socialists, believing that socialism is inevitable but that it has to be striven for, have taken Marxism as a program of action and have concentrated their efforts on political activity, leaving the problem of a socialist economy to be dealt with at the appropriate time.

It is not too much to say that orthodox economists, that is, economists of the school of Marshall and of the Austrian and Lausanne schools, are in part responsible for the poverty of thought concerning the economics of socialism. Holding that the proper field of economic theory is the field of pure abstraction, where logic and mathematics can be rigorously applied, they have limited their analysis very largely to a condition of static equilibrium—a condition where change is ruled out and economic forces are in balance. As a result of this, they have given little attention to institutional considerations. Yet the institutions they have assumed have been almost exclusively capitalist. To have assumed capitalist institutions was only natural. In the first place, they have been brought up in a capitalist economy and, broadly speaking, are members of the dominant middle class; secondly, the capitalist economy has over the years approximated in some degree to their ideal economy.

The very position of the orthodox economist has discouraged inquiry into socialist economics, which, of course, is essentially an inquiry into economic institutions peculiar to socialism. So convinced, on the one hand, has the orthodox economist been of the irrelevance of institutional considerations that he has dismissed the problem of the evolution of capitalism as a matter for mere history, though a consideration of Marx's theory of capitalist evolution might have led him to a serious examination of socialism. So attached, on the other hand, has the orthodox economist been to capitalist institutions—to private ownership of the means of production and to private enterprise—that he has not shown that his main theories would apply equally well to a capitalist and a socialist economy. Again, so attached has he been that he has not considered whether socialist institutions might permit a closer approximation to his ideal economy, though theoretically this would certainly be the case. Orthodox economists, we suggest, have given little attention to socialist economics either because they have been absorbed in the realm of pure theory or because they have been devoted to capitalist institutions.

It should be said at once that the above criticism applies to orthodox economists as a group and not to all orthodox economists, for there have been exceptions. The first to show that the formal principles of economic theory would apply to a socialist economy was an orthodox economist, Pareto. The first to work out Pareto's ideas and to demonstrate that the formal principles of economic theory would apply to a socialist economy was Barone, an orthodox economist of the Lausanne school (Walras and Pareto). Fred Taylor, an orthodox economist, was the first to show how a socialist economy could work in practice. And Frank Knight, an orthodox economist, has pointed out that orthodox economic theory would apply to a socialist as well as to a capitalist economy.

And now Pigou, who is one of the greatest living theoretical economists and whose very person embodies the whole Marshallian tradition, has recently come to the conclusion that a socialist economy is theoretically possible and is possible in practice, though "extraordinarily difficult" to work out. His *Socialism versus Capitalism*[2] holds that a socialist economy, on the ground of economic technique, is superior in most respects to a capitalist. It is significant, indeed, that the leader of orthodox economics has given a sympathetic exposition of socialism, in fact, has taken the position of a Fabian socialist, and has even warned against the chief danger of Fabianism. He remarks that "gradualness" is not a polite name for standing still.

II

Whatever may be the explanation for the widespread belief that socialism is impracticable, we are concerned here with whether or not socialism is workable from the economic angle. The problem of a socialist economy is twofold. First, will the authorities of a socialist economy dictate what products consumers shall buy or will consumers dictate to the authorities, as is the case more or less under capitalism? In more technical language, will there be free consumers' choice? Secondly, can resources be put to work so that the most will be made of them, that is, can resources be economized? In more technical language, is a rational allocation of resources possible in a socialist economy?

[2] Published in London in the fall of 1937, after these essays had been brought together for publication.

The first problem is, of course, easily solved; a socialist economy by definition presupposes free consumers' choice. A socialist economy in the classical sense is one that socializes production alone, as contrasted with communism, which socializes both production and consumption. The contributors to this volume, Taylor and Lange, deal with a socialist economy in the classical sense. Both assume freedom of choice in consumption and freedom of choice in occupation. Therefore, it naturally follows for these writers that the preferences of consumers, as expressed by their demand prices (the prices they are prepared to pay for a product), are the guiding criteria of production, and ultimately of the allocation of resources. Thus the citizens of a socialist state will virtually dictate what commodities the authorities shall produce, and in substantially the same way as the citizens of a capitalist state dictate what private industry shall produce.

The solution of the second problem is much more difficult; in fact, the problem of a rational allocation of resources is the central problem of socialist economics. In order to solve this problem a knowledge of the relative (or comparative) importance of the primary factors of production, such as land, minerals, water power, and various kinds of labor services, is crucial. At bottom the problem of a rational allocation of resources is one of valuation, of ascertaining the relative economic significance of the primary factors of production. We must be able to valuate these factors, even though it cannot be done very accurately, if we are to make calculations in regard to them. Economic calculation is necessary if the most appropriate use is to be made of scarce resources.

A knowledge of the primary factors of production is necessary, for example, if we are to calculate how much of one factor should be used in making a product as compared with another; for example, in manufacturing a railroad coach, how much steel as compared with aluminum. Again, a knowledge of the primary factors is necessary if we are to know when to substitute one product for another, when to replace a steam locomotive with a Diesel. Economic calculation is indispensable if we are to minimize costs in combining the factors of production, and if we are to see that the selling price of a product covers its cost; in other words, if we are to be economical in the use of our scarce resources. Without economic calculation there must be a great misdirection of resources and enormous waste. A society that does not employ economic calculation is condemned to a low standard of living.

The virtue of a competitive economy is that it makes a more or less rational allocation of resources. Under a competitive economy, the primary factors of production are valued on a market, where buyers and sellers bid with and against each other for the hire of these factors; the prices that they establish represent what all the buyers and sellers, taken together, believe the factors to be worth. These prices are economically significant, that is, they indicate the relative importance of the factors; they reflect the value placed on them by men who, under the pressure of competition, are striving to be economical in order to maximize profit. As a result of competition for profit, a competitive economy tends to do two things: to minimize costs and to make the selling price of the product equal to the cost of producing it. This tendency is the great merit of a competitive economy. Any economy that would rival a competitive one must show that there is a reasonable presumption that it will do these same two things. Otherwise there is no reason to believe that it will economize its resources.

Professor von Mises, the well-known Viennese economist and the leading opponent of socialism among economic thinkers, has argued vigorously that a rational allocation of resources is impossible in a socialist state on the ground that public ownership of the instruments of production does away with a market for capital goods. It follows for Mises that where there is no market for capital goods, there can be no prices for them; and without prices, which indicate the relative importance of the factors of production, economic calculation (or economic accounting) is out of the question.

Oskar Lange, in this volume, shows that Mises is able to deny the existence of prices in the capital goods industries of a socialist state by confusing the nature of prices. Lange argues that if prices are looked at not in the narrow (and ordinary) sense of the word as exchange ratios on a market (or the money for which a material thing or service can be obtained), but in the generic sense of "terms on which alternatives are offered," then there is no difficulty for socialism. For the absence of a market does not prevent the setting up of accounting prices or provisional valuations for the purpose of allocating resources.

Clearly it would not be difficult for a socialist state to set up accounting prices in the capital goods industries; the real problem is whether the accounting prices would be economically significant or quite arbitrary. Mises holds that these prices would be arbitrary—on the ground, of course, that there is no market for capital goods and therefore that the goods cannot be priced. Even G. D. H. Cole, a socialist writer, holds that accounting prices would be arbitrary.

Though Mises has been challenging the socialists since 1920, his argument had really been disproved early in the century by Barone, an Italian economist. In his notable essay, "The Ministry of Production in the Collectivist State," written in 1908, Barone proved that in principle the accounting prices of a socialist economy would be as economically significant as the market prices of a competitive economy. By a mathematical demonstration using simultaneous equations, Barone, following suggestions of Pareto, was the first to demonstrate that it was possible for a socialist economy to make a rational allocation of resources. His analysis showed, moreover, the great formal similarity of a socialist regime to a competitive one; indeed, he maintained that production in a socialist regime would be ordered in substantially the same way as it was in a competitive one. Barone's paper was pathfinding. And apparently it served to turn the flank of the attack of orthodox economics.

Professors Hayek and Robbins of the London School of Economics, who next to Mises are the leading opponents of socialism among economists, have apparently been influenced by Barone. They have taken up a second line of attack, the line that is usually taken after a principle has been admitted. They admit that a rational allocation of resources is theoretically possible in a socialist state, but deny that it can be worked out in practice. They insist that in order to determine prices the Central Planning Board of a socialist state would have to have "complete lists of the different quantities of all commodities which would be bought at any possible combination of prices of the different commodities that might be available." They also argue that the Central Planning Board would have to solve thousands, even millions, of calculations—simultaneous equations—before economic decisions could be taken, and with any means known at present these calculations could not be solved in a lifetime.

"The Guidance of Production in a Socialist State," the second paper in this volume, provides in substance the answer to the contention of Hayek and Robbins. Written by the late Professor Fred M. Taylor in 1928, before Hayek and Robbins had made their attack, this is the first writing to mark an advance on Barone's contribution. Though Barone indicated that it was possible to solve the calculations necessary to a rational allocation of resources in a socialist economy by a method of trial and error, he did not show how such a method could be carried out.

It was left to Taylor to point this out. The crucial problem is to determine the relative importance (what Taylor calls the "effective importance") of the primary factors of production. According to Taylor, the relative importance of each primary factor is derived from and determined by the importances of the innumerable commodities which emerge from the whole complex of productive processes. The question is, how in a concrete way is the relative importance of each factor determined? Taylor's answer is that a provisional valuation, in terms of money, would be assigned to each factor. The managers of the socialist industries would then carry on their operations as if the provisional valuations were absolutely correct.

Then, if the authorities had assigned a valuation to any particular factor which was too high or too low, that fact would be disclosed in unmistakable ways. If too high an evaluation had been assigned, causing the authorities to be unduly economical in the use of that factor, a physical surplus would show at the end of the productive period. If too low an evaluation had been assigned, leading the authorities to be too lavish in the use of that factor, a deficit would show. Surplus or deficit—one or the other would result from every wrong valuation of a factor. By successive trials the correct valuation for each factor, showing its relative importance, could be found. In other words, by a method of trial and error the correct accounting price for each factor could be ascertained.

Lange, writing after Hayek and Robbins had made their attack, answers them directly, using Taylor's analysis as the basis of his argument. He shows their position to be unreal by pointing out that the method of trial and error for determining accounting prices in a socialist economy would be substantially the same as that by which prices are actually determined on a competitive market. The Central Planning Board, he says, would not need to have, as Hayek seems to think, complete lists of the different quantities of all commodities which would be bought at any possible combination of prices of the different quantities which might be available. "Neither would the Central Planning Board have to solve hundreds of thousands of equations. The only 'equations' which would have to be 'solved' would be those of the consumers and the managers of production. These are exactly the same 'equations' which are solved in the present economic system and the persons who do the 'solving' are the same also. . . . And only a few of them have been graduated in higher mathematics. Professor Hayek and Professor Robbins 'solve' at least hundreds of equations daily, for instance, in buying a newspaper or in deciding to take a meal in a restaurant, and presumably they do not use determinates or Jacobians for the purpose."

Thus Lange argues that neither mathematics nor a knowledge of the demand and supply functions is needed in finding out the "right" accounting prices. The "right" accounting prices are "simply found by watching the quantities demanded and the quantities supplied and by raising the price of a commodity or service whenever there is an excess of demand over supply and lowering it whenever the reverse is the case, until, by trial and error, the price is found at which demand and supply are in balance." It may be remarked that it is important to arrive at, or approximate, this "right" (equilibrium) price in order that there is neither a misdirection of resources and waste on the producer's (the supply) side, nor a maldistribution of wants on the consumer's (the demand) side.

As we have said, Lange shows that a socialist economy would determine accounting prices in substantially the same way as prices are determined on a competitive market under capitalism. He does this not only by explaining that a socialist economy, like a capitalist, would use a method of trial and error, but also by pointing out that it would use this method under fundamentally the same conditions as it is used under capitalism. Under capitalism, he says, the method of trial and error is based above all on what he calls the *parametric function of prices,* i.e., on the fact that although the prices which confront the individual businessman are the result of the decisions of all individuals on the market, each individual regards the actual market prices as given data to which he has to adjust himself.

Each individual businessman tries to exploit the market situation which confronts him and which he cannot control.

A price structure, Lange insists, as objective or as economically significant as one under competitive capitalism can be obtained in a socialist economy if the parametric function of prices is retained. Under a socialist economy the parametric function of prices would be imposed as an accounting rule, and all decisions and all accounting of individual plant managers would be made as if prices were independent of the decisions taken. For purposes of accounting, plant managers would treat prices as constant, just as they are treated by businessmen under the competitive system.

We saw above that the virtue of a competitive market was the tendency of businessmen to minimize costs in combining the factors of production and to make the selling price cover the cost of the product. How are these two things to be achieved in a socialist economy? Lange's answer is that they must be laid down as working rules, as necessary conditions under which plant managers are to carry on production.

Thus the process of price determination in a socialist economy is quite like that in a competitive one. The Central Planning Board performs the functions of the market. It establishes the same essential conditions: the parametric use of prices in accounting; and the two essential rules—minimization of costs and equality of marginal cost and selling price of the product—for combining the factors of production, for choosing the scale of output of a plant, and for determining the output of an industry. The Central Planning Board enables the socialist economy to ascertain the relative importance of the factors of production and to make a rational allocation of resources.

It may be asked, would the Central Planning Board in the very beginning set the first accounting prices purely by guesswork? The answer is, no. The Central Planning Board would begin with prices *historically given,* about which we have considerable information. The board would have as much knowledge if not a great deal more information than business now has. Adjustments of the historically given prices would constantly be made, and there would be no need, as might be thought, of building up an entirely new price system.

If much the same forces would operate a socialist system as operate the competitive, it may reasonably be asked, why change to a socialist? Lange answers this question by arguing that a socialist economy is superior in two important ways. In the first place, he says, it is superior on the ground that it could reach the right equilibrium prices (prices which balance supply and demand) by a much shorter succession of trials than a competitive market actually does. It could do this for the simple reason that the Central Planning Board would have a much wider knowledge of what is going on in the economic system as a whole than any private entrepreneur can possibly have under capitalism. As Dickinson puts it, the system would work, as it were, in a glass house in which all the details of the mechanism and its working could be followed.

With greater knowledge of the economic system as a whole, Lange continues, the Central Planning Board could more properly take into account all the alternatives sacrificed and realized in production. The most important alternatives, like life, security, and health of the workers, are, under private enterprise, sacrificed without being accounted for. A socialist economy could, on the other hand, undoubtedly go a long way toward evaluating these social costs. As a result, a socialist economy would be able to avoid much of the social waste associated with private enterprise.

Still more important, a socialist economy, as a result of taking into account the various alternatives, would not be subject to the fluctuations of the business cycle; at least severe depressions and great unemployment would not be likely to occur. Of course, grave mistakes would undoubtedly be made in a socialist economy, such as misdirection of investments and production; but such mistakes would not necessarily involve the whole economic system in a general shrinkage of output and unemployment of factors of production. The merit of a socialist economy is that mistakes can be *localized,* a partial overproduction need not turn into a general one. There is no need to correct losses in one part of the economy, as is done under capitalism, by a procedure that creates in other parts still further losses by the secondary effect of a cumulative shrinkage of demand and of unemployment of the factors of production.

The second important way, continues Lange, in which a socialist economy is superior to a capitalist is in the distribution of incomes. A socialist economy, he maintains, can so distribute incomes as to maximize social welfare, while the capitalist economy that we know or are likely to know can never hope to do so. For under capitalism incomes are distributed according to the ownership of the means of production; and these are privately owned by the few, while the mass of men own nothing but their labor power. Under such conditions, demand price (or what consumers are willing and able to pay) does not reflect the relative urgency of needs of different persons. On the contrary, it reflects the incomes of many who go without necessities and the incomes of the few who go in luxury. Thus at the present time the allocation of resources as determined by the demand price offered for consumer's goods is far from attaining the maximum of social welfare.

Lange argues that if incomes are to be distributed so as to maximize the social welfare two conditions must be satisfied. First, the same demand price offered by different consumers must represent an equal urgency of need. Second, the services of labor must be apportioned among the different occupations so that the value of the marginal product of labor equals the marginal disutility involved in pursuing these occupations. In other words, that the product which results from adding the last unit of labor that just pays for itself is equal to the discomfort or pain necessary to produce it. It may appear, he says, that there is a contradiction between the first and second conditions; that the first requires the distribution of equal incomes, and the second unequal incomes. But the contradiction is only apparent. By putting such things as leisure, safety, and agreeableness of work into the utility scales of the individuals, the disutility of any occupation can be represented as an opportunity cost. An occupation offering a lower money income, and a smaller disutility, may be interpreted as the purchase of leisure, safety, and agreeableness of work at a price equal to the difference of the money income earned in that particular occupation and in others. Instead of attaching to the various occupations different incomes, the administration of a socialist economy might pay to any citizen the same money income and charge a price for the pursuit of each occupation.

There can be no doubt that a socialist economy could adequately satisfy these two conditions, whereas capitalism cannot possibly do so. A socialist economy, as Lange puts it, could base the distribution of income on the assumption that individuals have the same marginal utility curve of income, and could strike the right average in estimating the relative urgency of the needs of different persons, leaving only random errors; whereas the distribution of income in a capitalist society introduces a constant error— a class error in favor of the rich.

Against these advantages of a socialist economy Lange sets the disadvantage of an arbitrary rate of capital accumulation. It is obvious that a socialist economy must set aside capital for maintenance and new investments, in order not only to maintain its present industries in good working condition, but also to bring in technical innovations and to create new industries so that the standard of living can be raised. For these purposes capital must be accumulated and in order to do this a price, that is to say, interest, must be charged for the use of capital. What is important to decide is the rate of interest, or the speed at which capital shall accumulate. This rate cannot be determined by consumers' preferences, as it is under capitalism, for most of the capital is owned by the government and controlled by government banks. That the rate of interest will be determined not by consumers deciding how much to save but arbitrarily by the Central Planning Board may be considered, Lange says, a diminution of social welfare.

Yet he believes that from the economic angle it is doubtful whether a rate of interest reflecting consumers' preferences is superior to one set arbitrarily by the Central Planning Board. He says that we must distinguish between the short period and the long. In respect to the short period, under both capitalism and socialism, the amount of capital is regarded as constant and the rate of interest is determined simply by the condition that the demand for capital is equal to the amount available. Here, as before, the Central Planning Board would undoubtedly begin with a rate based upon historically given rates and adjust this rate by a process of trial and error until the "correct" rate was attained. Such a procedure would be substantially the same as that at present followed under the capitalist economy.

The main difference, however, between a capitalist and a socialist economy occurs in respect to the long period. Under a socialist economy the rate is set, as we have said, arbitrarily by the Central Planning Board; yet it is by no means certain that a rate reflecting consumers' preferences is superior. Lange argues that in the present economic order saving is only partly determined by utility considerations; the rate of saving, he affirms, is affected much more by the distribution of incomes, which is irrational from the economist's point of view. It is also true, he says, that in a capitalist economy the public's attempt to save may be frustrated by not being followed by an appropriate rate of investment; and poverty instead of increased wealth may result from the people's desire to save. Thus, under capitalism, too, the actual rate of capital accumulation is divorced from the preferences of the people; and the rate of capital accumulation determined "corporately" in a socialist society may from the economic point of view prove to be more rational than the actual rate of saving under capitalism. It is Lange's view that whatever may be the disadvantage in a socialist state of an arbitrary rate of interest, this disadvantage is overbalanced by the advantages.

The real problem, he believes, of a socialist state is not economic at all, but sociological; it is the problem of bureaucracy. The efficiency of public officials, he suggests, should be compared with that of corporation officials under capitalism, and not with the efficiency of private entrepreneurs as managers of production. If this is done, the argument that socialism means bureaucracy in industry loses much of its force. However, the bureaucratic management of economic life remains the real danger of socialism, though Lange does not see how the same or even greater danger can be averted under monopolistic capitalism.

It is not too much to say that the writings of Barone, Taylor, and Lange, and of others such as Dickinson and A. P. Lerner in England, A. R. Sweezy in America, and Heimann, Landauer, and Zassenhaus, formerly of Germany, have altered the terms of the debate between capitalism and socialism. The burden of proof has been shifted to the capitalist economy, which must now show why it should not be replaced by a socialist one, in view of its evident feasibility and superiority.

The burden of proof, however, has been shifted not only because of the argument outlined above, but also because the real issue is whether the further maintenance of the capitalist system will promote economic progress as rapidly as in the past. This issue will doubtless have more to do with whether a socialist economy will finally be developed than an analysis showing its superiority in theory and its feasibility in practice.

The capitalist economy today is as far from the pure ideal of the economic theorist as it is from a socialist economy. Large-scale enterprise has supplanted small-scale in a great part of the economy, with the result that competition has been seriously impaired. When competition is not in force, Lange points out, private enterprise is not compelled to introduce innovations—labor-saving devices, which are indispensable to increasing productivity—until the old capital invested is amortized. Of course, it will do so if the reduction in cost consequent upon introducing the innovation is so great as to offset the devaluation of the capital already invested. Under competition, on the other hand, where no single producer can influence prices and no single producer is powerful enough to prevent new firms from entering the industry, producers and investors *have* to submit to losses and devaluation of old investments resulting from innovations. They can counteract these effects only by introducing innovations themselves, which in turn inflict losses on others, yet promote economic progress.

When industries become so large that they can influence if not control prices and the entry of firms, they tend to avoid a devaluation of the capital invested as in the case of many Continental cartels. The tendency, moreover, to maintain the value of existing capital is accentuated by the divorce of ownership from control, which is a characteristic of most large-scale industry. For those who control large-scale industry must replace the value of the investment or fail. For these reasons, then, interventionism and restrictionism have become more and more the dominant economic policies of large-scale industry.

But, Lange says, the evil effects of oligopoly and monopolistic (or imperfect) competition do not stop here. For the introduction of innovations cannot be stopped altogether. When the pressure of new innovations becomes so strong that the artificially preserved value of the old investments is destroyed, the affected firms may break down completely. The increasing instability of capitalism can be remedied only by giving up the attempts to protect the value of old investments or by successfully stopping new innovations. "The capitalist system is faced with an unescapable dilemma: holding back technical progress leads, through the exhaustion of profitable investment opportunities, to a state of chronic unemployment which can be remedied only by a policy of public investments on an ever-increasing scale, while a continuance of technical progress leads to the instability due to the policy of protecting the value of old investments."

It should also be observed that large-scale industry and finance are politically significant. Because of their importance to the economy, they can use their power to obtain government intervention on their behalf. So long as the maximization of profit is the end of business activity, it will be natural for the large institutions to seek government intervention in order to increase profits or to increase the value of their investment.

If it is true, as Lange suggests, that the institutions of private ownership of the means of production and of private enterprise are ceasing to foster economic progress, that we are reaching or have reached a state in which these institutions are hindering instead of promoting technical development, then a socialist economy would seem to be the only solution. For it seems impossible, as a practical matter, that we could actually break up large-scale monopolistic enterprise in which competition is ineffective and return to a system of small-scale units with free competition. Nor would this really be desirable if it could be done, for it would mean giving up the great economic advantages of mass production, which are technically inseparable from the large unit. It goes without saying that a great deal of advanced technology would be absolutely excluded from an artificially maintained system of free competition.

The other way, Lange points out, in which the difficulties of capitalism might be solved within the framework of private ownership is by government control of production and investment for the purpose of preventing monopoly and restrictionism. Yet this solution is hardly more promising than the first. For, if the past history of regulation and partial control is pertinent, huge corporations, in virtue of their great economic power, would be more likely to control the government than the government the corporations. Control by corporations would result in planning for monopoly and restrictionism, which would defeat the original purpose for which control was undertaken. But even if this could be avoided, it is unlikely that such control would be successful.

To retain the main characteristics of capitalism—private property, private enterprise, and the pursuit of maximum profit—and to force business to do things which are contrary to its way of life would only confuse business and set it against itself. To regiment investment and enterprise, and to compel actual losses of capital in order to prevent overvaluation of investments would sooner or later bring about the paralysis of business. Thus the government would have either to yield and give up any effective interference with the pursuit of maximum profit, or to place under government ownership and management the defiant corporations. This latter course would lead straight to socialism.

It is clear for Lange that the defects of present-day capitalism—monopoly, restrictionism, and interventionism—can be done away with only by adopting a socialist economy. For him a socialist economy, however, does not mean the complete abolition of private enterprise and private ownership of production. He believes that private enterprise and private ownership of the means of production should be kept in fields where competition is effective, i.e., in small-scale industry and farming.

Not the least interesting part of Lange's discussion is his analysis of the problem of transition from a capitalist to a socialist economy. He takes issue with the orthodox view of economic gradualism, which is found not only among right-wing socialists but also among left-wing socialists and among communists. While the latter two regard a rapid socialization as necessary on the ground of political strategy, they generally hold that on the ground of economic considerations a gradual socialization is preferable to a rapid one. Lange takes the opposite view and argues that gradual socialization cannot be successful. The attempt, he says, of a socialist government to force businessmen to act differently from the way demanded by the pursuit of profit would at best cause constant friction, and most likely breakdown.

The very existence, he remarks, of a socialist government bent on socialization is a constant threat to the security of a capitalist economy. An economic system based upon private enterprise and private ownership of the means of production cannot hope to function adequately if its foundations are insecure. Men who are faced with the threat of expropriation can have little inducement to manage their business efficiently, let alone to invest in it or to improve it. If a socialist government socializes the coal mines today and declares that it will socialize the textile industry tomorrow, the textile industry will most likely be ruined before it will be socialized.

Lange concludes that a socialist government really intent upon socialization has to carry out its program at one stroke or give it up altogether. Since the coming to power of a socialist party in a capitalist society would most likely bring about a financial panic and economic collapse, a socialist government must either socialize at once or cease to be a socialist government. Socialism, he remarks, is not an economic policy for the timid.

Lange believes not only that monopolistic, basic, and natural resources industries should be taken over at one stroke, but that the socialist government should guarantee the security of private property and enterprise not explicitly included in the socialization measures. He says that it should be made absolutely clear to everybody that socialization is not directed against private property as such, but only against that special type of private property that creates obstacles to economic progress and is the parent of privilege. All private property of the means of production and all private enterprise that serve a *useful social function* should enjoy the full protection and support of the socialist state.

Lange thinks, however, that there may be special situations in which a socialist party may assume power on a program other than that of comprehensive socialization. The special situations are those with which a capitalist party is unable to cope. He cites as an example a situation of unemployment and depression in which a bold program of public investment is needed and a capitalist party is unwilling to embark upon such a program because the low rate of return is a violation of the principle that investments ought to be made only for profit. He suggests that in such a situation a socialist party might come to power on a "labor plan" and restore the health of the capitalist economy. If successful, its position would be greatly strengthened. Thus, he says, a labor plan might prove an important link in the transition between a capitalist and socialist economy. Yet a socialist party must carry out even a labor plan with boldness and decision, else it becomes the mere administrator of the existing capitalist society, a function which it must necessarily perform much less effectively than a capitalist party.

III

The task remains to point out briefly the bearing of Taylor's and Lange's essays on the problem of government control of the economic order. First and foremost, these essays remove the economic objection to a socialist state. They show, from the point of view of the economist, that a socialist economy is a rational economy, and that it is possible not only in theory but also in practice. The essays show, in contradiction to popular thought, that there is nothing inherent in a socialist economy that requires an autocratic system of government, nor that would impair democracy. On the contrary, a socialist economy is far more in harmony with democracy than is a capitalist.

The genius of democracy, Matthew Arnold observed, is equality; by this he meant that the thrust of democracy is toward the removal of privilege, of artificial inequalities that cannot be justified in terms of the common welfare. The privilege that exists today in democratic states is based largely on wealth, and rests at bottom on capitalist arrangements, on the private ownership of the means of production. A socialist economy would eliminate the privilege that arises from wealth, since it stands for an equal distribution of income. Democracy's aim is to govern in the interests of the whole community; therefore democracy stands, in principle, for the satisfaction of necessities before luxuries. A socialist economy stands for this same principle, for equality in the distribution of income means that needs will be satisfied in proportion to their urgency.

If equality is a fundamental characteristic of democracy, so also is liberty. In this regard also a socialist economy is more in harmony with democracy than a capitalist, for, with a more equal distribution of income, free consumer's choice would be still freer. Where many under a capitalist economy must choose between a coat and a pair of shoes, under a socialist many could choose between a radio and a telephone.

It will doubtless be argued that public ownership of a great segment of industry is the high road to dictatorship. The corollary of this argument is that private ownership is a bulwark against tyranny. The immediate comment on these arguments must be that the form of property ownership of itself, whether public or private, neither promotes nor hinders freedom. What is crucial is the character of the authority which administers it, or the way in which the property is controlled.

Under feudal arrangements, private ownership went hand in hand with a local tyranny that was only mitigated by the rise of monarchy and the establishment of a central power. The lesson of this change is that a central authority, even though autocratic, proved to be less arbitrary locally than private autocracy. At the present time the very place where tyranny exists in democratic states is in privately owned industry; here power is exercised autocratically and often ruthlessly. To be sure, private ownership of the means of production prevents government from tyrannizing over industry; at the same time, it enables industry to dominate government and to tyrannize over workers. In view of this condition of things, government ownership of basic industry carried out by a democratic government offers a means of taking autocracy out of industry.

The reason men resort to public ownership is for the purpose of obtaining more responsible action. Toll roads, for example, were abolished because private management broke down. Government ownership and management of roads, it may be observed, has led to greater freedom, and government ownership and management of the postal service and electrical power has hardly led to tyranny. It is perfectly true that the administration of an industry, like the administration of a social service such as the department of health, must be organized to a considerable extent on the autocratic principle. But the socialization of industry under a democracy would mean that the autocratic principle would be tempered by the introduction of democratic methods of assuring responsible action and by the establishment of decent working conditions. It goes without saying that the democratic methods introduced must be compatible with efficiency.

Democratizing administrative authority in industry would involve bringing in constitutional ways of life for whole industries and effective consultation between workers and management. To consult men who live under and feel the results of rules and administrative action, to attach importance to their experience in this regard, and to represent it appropriately in the bodies that frame the rules which affect them must raise the moral tone and the morale of the whole working community. A socialized industry would work in an atmosphere of publicity; records would be open to the public. Few things would make for responsibility more surely than this. Where industry is publicly owned, measurement, however rough, is possible; this would make for efficiency as well as for responsibility.

In a socialized state industry would become a profession; that is, for positions requiring special training a show of qualification would be demanded of applicants, and openings would be filled on the competitive principle. A man's personnel record and not, as is so frequently the case today, the influence of his friends or the personality of his property would determine his position and responsibility. And this would be the case not only for entrance into positions but also for advancement. Thus in the socialized industries, as in the professions, the setting of standards would be a means of discovering excellence, and the existence of standards would act as a check on personal power. And in all positions a personnel policy that made room for flexibility would be substituted for a personal policy.

It will probably be argued that a Central Planning Board involves a dangerous concentration of power. There can be no doubt that the Central Planning Board would exercise great power, but would it be any greater than that exercised collectively by private boards of directors? Because the decisions of private boards are made here and there, this does not mean that the consumer does not feel their collective impact, even though it may take a depression to make him aware of it. The problem is not the form of the power, but whether it is exercised responsibly. There is reason to believe that it could be exercised more responsibly under a Central Planning Board than under private industry, for the first would operate with greater knowledge. Government has unrivaled access to the facts and unrivaled resources for their collection.

Nor would the Central Planning Board be the sovereign authority of the state. If it were not made up of members of the executive, which might be the best solution, it would be appointed by the executive and directly responsible to it. However it might be composed and appointed, it would be responsible to the legislature for general policy. Associated with the Central Planning Board would be a technical staff which would report on resources, supplies, deficits, and prices and carry on research and suggest economic policies. It would be removed, within reasonable limits, from political influence, that is, its chiefs would be semi-permanent, appointed by the executive for a ten- or fifteen-year period always with the possibility of renewal of the appointment. Nor would the Central Planning Board and its technical staff do all the planning. This function would to a great extent be decentralized. There would be regional and local planning boards and technical staffs. The Central Planning Board would co-ordinate data and plans of the subordinate boards; it would suggest to the executive plans for the economy as a whole.

Lange's discussion of income distribution is especially instructive for socialist writers who approach the problem of reward from the social and ethical angle. He fully appreciates, of course, the socialist stand for equality of income; that equality is essential if the demands of different consumers for commodities at the same price are to represent an equal urgency of need. At the same time he shows that a practical solution must involve an element of inequality; that a differential in remuneration is necessary if labor services are to be apportioned in the most advantageous way economically. Lange presents, as we saw above, an ingenious solution for this apparent conflict in principle. His solution enables the socialist's insistence on equality to be satisfied, and the demand of the economist that there be an equilibrium between the marginal productivity of labor and the relative marginal disutility of work.

It would seem that Lange is right in holding that bureaucracy is the real danger in a socialist economy. The chief danger is, as with any large-scale organization, whether public or private, a resistance to novelty, an aversion to innovation. That a socialist industry would work in a climate of publicity, consultation, criticism, and measurement would make it more amenable than private monopoly to experiment, though special effort would still have to be made to maintain flexibility and openness to new ideas. As Frank Knight has said, the problem of a socialist economy is not an economic problem but a political and sociological one.

Socialists often say that a socialist economy would eliminate the enormous waste that characterizes capitalism. It seems reasonable to hold that a socialist economy could avoid a considerable amount of the waste that occurs under capitalism, yet it could hardly avoid waste. Nor should it strive to do so, for there is such a thing as necessary waste; that which is the product of experiment. As Barone pointed out, a socialist economy must experiment and therefore must incur waste, else it will be impossible to determine whether the best use is being made of available resources. And unless this is done the standard of living cannot be raised.

Lange's discussion of the problem of transition from a capitalist to a socialist economy would seem to be irrefutable, and should compel socialists and communists to rethink their stock notions. His suggestion for a labor plan, which seems to reflect the experience of Sweden, might make possible the achievement of that rare thing in history—a fundamental change in political control, or in class relations, without a conflict.

THE GUIDANCE OF PRODUCTION
IN A SOCIALIST STATE

Fred M. Taylor

THE GUIDANCE OF PRODUCTION IN
A SOCIALIST STATE

By FRED M. TAYLOR

LIKE most teachers of economic theory, I have found it quite worth while to spend some time studying any particular problem in hand from the standpoint of a socialist state. In fact I have more than once found it profitable to work out, from that standpoint, a quite specific solution of the problem in question—setting up as the proper criterion of a sound solution that it should seem entirely reasonable in view of the essential nature of a socialist state. Herein, I am applying this method of procedure to a very fundamental problem of any co-operative economic order, that is, the problem embodied in this question: What is the proper method of determining just what commodities shall be produced from the economic resources at the disposal of a given community?

Under the present economic order of free private initiative, the actual decision as to what commodities shall be produced is made very simply. First, on the basis of a vast complex of institutions, customs, and laws, the citizen adopts a line of conduct which provides him with a money

Presidential address delivered at the forty-first annual meeting of the American Economic Association, Chicago, Illinois, December 27, 1928. Reprinted from the *American Economic Review*, Vol. 19, No. 1 (March, 1929).

income of greater or lesser volume. Secondly, that citizen comes on the market with said income demanding from those persons who have voluntarily assumed the role of producers whatever commodities he, the citizen, chooses. Thirdly, the producers promptly submit to the dictation of the citizen in this matter, provided always that said citizen brings along with his demand entire readiness to pay for each commodity a price equal to the cost of producing that commodity. In the case of a socialist state, the proper method of determining what commodities shall be produced would be in outline substantially the same as that just described. That is, the correct general procedure would be this: (1) The state would assure to the citizen a given money income and (2) the state would authorize the citizen to spend that income as he chose in buying commodities produced by the state—a procedure which would virtually authorize the citizen to dictate just what commodities the economic authorities of the state should produce.

This paper, taken as a whole, is a defense of the method of guiding production in a socialist state which has just been described. But that defense really breaks into two parts. The first part of this paper is used in making the direct defense, that is, in setting forth the specific reasons why that method is essentially sound. The second part will be used to deal with a subordinate problem, that is, a problem which would have to be solved by the authorities before the plan for guiding production here advocated could be followed. The specific nature of this subordinate problem will be more easily brought out a little later.

So much for the two tasks with which we are to deal in this paper. Before starting upon those tasks, we must take a moment to explain just what meaning will attach to the phrase "socialist state" as used in this paper. A state so designated is here understood as being one in which the control of the whole apparatus of production and the guidance of all productive operations is to be in the hands of the state itself. In other words, the state is to be the sole responsible producer, that is, the sole person, natural or legal, who is authorized to employ the economic resources of the community, its stock or income of primary factors, in producing commodities. As such sole producer, the state maintains exchange relations with its citizens, buying their productive services with money and selling to them the commodities which it produces.

I

Keeping in mind this conception of a socialist state, we must now take up our first task, that is, the task of defending the proposition already laid down, that in a socialist state the proper method of determining what commodities should be produced would be to assure each citizen a money income and then to authorize that citizen to call on the state to produce the particular commodities which he—the citizen—wanted. Here our first step must be to note some details which would be included in our plan.

In the first place, when we describe the proper method of determining what commodities shall be produced as being a method which begins by assuring to each citizen a certain money income, it is of course assumed that said income is assured to the citizen only with the proviso that certain conditions fixed by the state have been fulfilled. Just what these conditions ought to be we must not take time to consider; but that conditions of some sort should be attached to the receiving of an income cannot be questioned.

Another detail of our plan which is assumed is that, in determining the money incomes to be conditionally assured to the citizens of a socialist state, the authorities of such a state would have honestly and earnestly endeavored to fix those incomes so that they represent that distribution of the total income of the state which is called for in the interest of citizens generally and of the group as an organic whole. This socially correct system of incomes being assumed, it necessarily follows that the judgments reached by citizens with respect to the relative importances of different commodities would be virtually social judgments, and the resulting commodity prices would be prices which expressed the social importances of commodities.

A third specific provision which is assumed to be present in the socialist plan for determining what commodities to produce is this: In deciding whether or not to demand the production of a particular commodity, the citizen must have before his mind just what price he would be obliged to pay for that commodity. Such a provision would be indispensable, since the citizen would not be able to reach a decision as to whether or not he wanted to buy a given commodity unless he had before him the data necessary for comparing the desirability of said commodity with the drain on his income which the buying of that commodity would involve.

The last specific provision of the correct socialist plan for dealing with our problem would be this: In fixing the selling price of any particular commodity, the economic authorities would set that price at a point which fully covered the cost of producing said commodity, and those authorities would understand the cost of producing that commodity to be the drain on the economic resources of the community—its stock or income of primary factors—consequent upon producing said commodity.

As the particular procedure brought out in the last sentence plays an essential part in making the plan for guiding production advocated in this paper the right plan, I must add here two or three comments. First, by the phrase "primary factors" is meant those economic factors of production behind which the economist does not attempt to go, for example, the land itself, the water powers, the original raw materials such as metallic ores, the different kinds of labor services, etc.

Again, by the phrase "effective importance" I mean the degree of importance which is a resultant of the whole situation, particularly of the generic importance of the factor in question and the quantity of it available. Put in another way, the effective importance of anything is that degree of importance which we should take into account in deciding how to act. Thus, a man sitting beside a flowing well has no occasion to economize in the use of water; and so in this situation water to him has no effective importance. To the same man, however, if temporarily lost in the desert with his whole stock of water reduced to a single quart, the utmost possible economy in the use of water would be imperative; and the effective importance of his stock of water would be beyond estimate.

A third comment needed here is that each one of these numerous primary factors has its own particular degree or amount of effective importance in the vast complex of productive processes in which it participates. That effective importance of each primary factor is derived from and determined by the importances of the innumerable commodities which emerge from that complex of productive processes. Because the effective importances of the commodities are expressed in terms of money value, the importances of the several factors will be so expressed. At present it will be assumed—to prove this assumption will be the task of the second part of this paper—that the authorities of our socialist state will have proved able to ascertain with a sufficient degree of accuracy these effective importances or values of all the different kinds of primary factors, and that they will have embodied the results in arithmetic tables which I shall usually designate factor-valuation tables. In order to determine the cost of producing any particular commodity, let us say a sewing machine, it would be necessary to multiply the valuation of each factor used in producing that machine by the quantity of that factor so used and add together these different products. If the resultant total turned out to be thirty dollars, we should have to say that the producing of the sewing machine made a drain on the community's economic resources amounting to thirty dollars; or, in other words, that its resources-cost was thirty dollars.

I must not leave this matter of cost in a socialist state without remarking that the kind of cost just explained, resources-cost, is in fact very closely allied to what in our system is often called expense-cost. Indeed, a very good case can be made for the contention that, in the present order, these two kinds of cost are essentially the same thing, though capable of being looked at, and labeled, from two quite different points of view. To the voluntary producer of our present order, who must buy the factors which he uses to produce a sewing machine, the thirty-dollar cost of producing that sewing machine is an expense-cost. On the other hand, to the economist who believes that the automatic working of competition gives to each primary factor a price which expresses with sufficient accuracy the effective importance of that factor in the productive process as a whole—to him that same thirty-dollar cost presents itself as a resources-cost, a drain on society's economic resources, of thirty dollars.

So much for the general character and the specific details of the plan for determining what commodities shall be produced, which I hold to be the only right plan for a socialist state to adopt. I must now take a few moments to argue for the soundness of the plan. In the first place, the plan in its general outline is surely the one which should be maintained in a socialist state. That is, (1) the state should determine the money income of the citizen; and (2) the citizen should dictate to the state what shall be produced in return for that income. The former provision would insure that the interests of citizens generally would not be sacrificed to the interests of particular individuals; the latter provision would insure that the peculiarities of tastes and needs characteristic of each individual would not be sacrificed to some standard of consumption set up by an all-powerful state.

I have argued that the proposed plan for guiding the production of commodities in a socialist state, viewed in its general outline, is essentially sound. As respects the more specific provisions of that plan which I have enumerated, I shall pass by the first three as needing no defense, and take up at once the fourth, which is the provision that the authorities of our socialist state, in fixing the price to be paid by the citizen for any particular commodity, ought to set that price at a point which covers completely the cost of producing that commodity, and that said authorities ought to interpret the cost of producing a given commodity to be its resources-cost, the drain on the community's store or income of primary factors which results from producing a unit of said commodity. Is this doctrine sound? Would it really be the correct thing for the authorities to fix the selling price of any commodity at cost in this sense?

To this question, the affirmative answer is surely the right one. A single consideration is decisive: That price which equals resources-cost is the only price which would be consistent with the income system supposed to have been already decided upon. That system, we remember, gives to each citizen a determinate money income to be employed as he sees fit in buying commodities from the state. But, since substantially all commodities which the citizen is permitted to buy, that is, consumption commodities, have to be produced, the authorities of the state, in deciding that a particular citizen shall have a certain money income—one, let us suppose, of two thousand dollars—have thereby virtually decided that said citizen shall have an incontestable claim upon two thousand dollars' worth of the productive resources of the state; and that proposition, in turn, means that said citizen shall have an incontestable right to dictate to the economic authorities just what commodities they shall produce from his two thousand dollars' worth of the productive resources of the community. From this reasoning it necessarily follows that the authorities could not consistently make the selling price of our hypothetical sewing machine greater than its resources-cost of thirty dollars, since doing so would in effect reduce the money income of the citizen interested, though it had previously been decided that said money income was just what it ought to be. On the other hand, it is equally evident that the authorities could not consistently make the selling price of the sewing machine smaller than its resources-cost of thirty dollars; since doing so would in effect increase the income of the citizen interested, though, by hypothesis, that income was already just what it ought to be.

II

In the preceding discussion, we have completed our main task, that is, the task of defending that method of procedure which I have set up as the only proper one to be followed by the authorities of a socialist state in deciding what commodities to produce. In the course of that discussion it has probably become sufficiently evident why it would be necessary for the authorities of our socialist state to solve the so-called problem of imputation, that is, the problem of ascertaining the effective importance in the productive process of each primary factor. Without that information, those authorities would manifestly be unable to compute the resources-cost of any particular commodity; hence would be unable to determine the correct selling price for that commodity; and consequently would be unable to make use of the particular method of determining just what commodities they ought to produce which, according to the contention of this paper, is the only correct method.

But not only would it be necessary for the authorities of a socialist state to solve this imputation problem as a prerequisite to the employment of this particular method of guiding production; it is not unlikely that more than one economist would question the possibility of solving that problem at all under the conditions necessarily prevailing in a socialist state. I seem called on, therefore, to give a few moments to show that, in fact, the socialist authorities would find themselves quite equal to this task.

The particular method of procedure which would seem most suitable for dealing with this problem in the case of a socialist state is a form of the so-called method of trial and error, that is, the method which consists in trying out a series of hypothetical solutions till one is found which proves a success.

As a necessary preliminary to the explanation of the process by which the method of trial and error could be used to solve the imputation problem, we must remind ourselves that at any particular time the stock or income of each primary factor which was available for the current production period would necessarily be a substantially determinate quantity. Unless the available quantity of any factor was thus determinate and at the same time so limited that its total was smaller than the need for that factor, though it might be a factor of production, it could not be an economic factor, and so could not be one of the factors with which we are concerned.

Now, setting out from this assumption that the quantity

of any economic factor which is available for any particular productive period is substantially determinate, I shall assume that the authorities of our socialist state, in trying to ascertain the effective importance of each primary factor, would adopt the following procedure: (1) They would set about constructing factor-valuation tables in which they would give each factor that valuation which, on the basis of much careful study, they believed to be the nearest approximation to its correct valuation that they could work out in advance of experience. (2) They would then proceed to carry on their functions as managers of all productive operations as if they considered the valuations given in their provisional tables to be the absolutely correct valuations. (3) While thus acting, they would after all keep a close watch for results which would indicate that some of their provisional valuations were incorrect. (4) If such results appeared, they would then make the needed corrections in the factor tables, lowering any valuations which had proved too high. raising any which had proved too low. (5) Finally, they would repeat this procedure until no further evidence of divergence from the correct valuations was forthcoming.

I hardly need say that the crucial stage in the above procedure is the third, that is, the stage during which the authorities would be on the watch to discover one or more indications that some of the valuations which they had put into the provisional tables were wrong—were too high or too low. Here the all-important question is this: Is it reasonable to expect that such indication would be forthcoming whenever particular factor valuations actually were too high or too low? The correct answer is surely an affirmative one. If, in regulating productive processes, the authorities were actually using for any particular factor a valuation which was too high or too low, that fact would soon disclose itself in unmistakable ways. Thus, supposing that, in the case of a particular factor, the valuation given in the provisional factor tables was too high, that fact would inevitably lead the authorities to be unduly economical in the use of that factor; and this conduct, in turn, would make the amount of that factor which was available for the current productive period larger than the amount which was consumed during that period. In other words, a too-high valuation of any factor would cause the stock of that factor to show a surplus at the end of the productive period.

If, now, we reverse our hypothesis and suppose that the valuation of a particular factor which appeared in the factor tables was too low, that fact would inevitably lead the authorities to be too lavish in the use of that factor; and this conduct, in turn, would result in making the amount of that factor available for the current productive period smaller than the amount needed during that period at the too-low valuation. In other words, a too-low valuation of any factor in the tables would be certain to cause a deficit in the stock of that factor. Surplus or deficit—one or the other would result from every wrong valuation of a factor.

From the above analysis it seems certain that the authorities of our socialist state would have no difficulty finding
out whether the standard valuation of any particular factor was too high or too low. And this much having been
learned, the rest would be easy. Those authorities would
now proceed to lower valuations which had proved too
high and raise those which had proved too low. Finally,
they would have no difficulty repeating this process until
neither a surplus nor a deficit appeared, when they would
rightly conclude that the valuation which was then attached to any particular factor correctly expressed the
effective importance of that factor. It follows that we can
now feel assured that said authorities would be able to
compute the resources-cost of producing any kind of commodity which the citizen might demand. But, since the
doubt on this point formed the principal ground for ques-
tioning the soundness of the main contention of this paper,
I find myself disposed to affirm rather dogmatically that,
if the economic authorities of a socialist state would recognize equality between cost of production on the one hand
and the demand price of the buyer on the other as being
the adequate and the only adequate proof that the commodity in question ought to be produced, they could, under all ordinary conditions, perform their duties, as the
persons who were immediately responsible for the guidance of production, with well-founded confidence that
they would never make any other than the right use of
the economic resources placed at their disposal.

ON THE ECONOMIC THEORY
OF SOCIALISM

Oskar Lange

ON THE ECONOMIC THEORY
OF SOCIALISM

By OSKAR LANGE

I. The Present State of the Debate

SOCIALISTS have certainly good reason to be grateful to Professor Mises, the great *advocatus diaboli* of their cause. For it was his powerful challenge that forced the socialists to recognize the importance of an adequate system of economic accounting to guide the allocation of resources in a socialist economy. Even more, it was chiefly due to Professor Mises' challenge that many socialists became aware of the very existence of such a problem. And although Professor Mises was not the first to raise it, and although not all socialists were as completely unaware of the problem as is frequently held, it is true, nevertheless, that, particularly on the European Continent (outside of Italy), the merit of having caused the socialists to approach this problem systematically belongs entirely to Professor Mises. Both as an expression of recognition for the great service rendered by him and as a memento of the prime importance of sound economic accounting, a statue of Professor Mises ought to occupy an honorable place in the great hall of the Ministry of Socialization or of the Cen-

Reprinted with additions and some changes from the *Review of Economic Studies,* Vol. IV, Nos. 1 and 2 (October, 1936, and February, 1937).

tral Planning Board of the socialist state. I am afraid, however, that Professor Mises would scarcely enjoy what seems the only adequate way to repay the debt of recognition incurred by the socialists, and it is difficult to blame him for not doing so. First, he might have to share his place with the great leaders of the socialist movement, and this company might not suit him. And then, to complete the misfortune, a socialist teacher might invite his students in a class on dialectical materialism to go and look at the statue, in order to exemplify the Hegelian *List der Vernunft* which made even the stanchest of bourgeois economists unwittingly serve the proletarian cause.

Since the clear and distinct formulation of a problem is certainly a major contribution to science, the economist will have to join the socialists in their recognition of Professor Mises' work on economic calculation in a socialist economy. As Professor Hayek has put it, to Professor Mises belongs "the distinction of having first formulated the central problem of socialist economics in such a form as to make it impossible that it should ever again disappear from the discussion."[1]

But, unfortunately, besides formulating the problem, Professor Mises has also claimed to have demonstrated that economic calculation is impossible in a socialist society.

[1] F. A. von Hayek, "The Nature and History of the Problem," Introduction to *Collectivist Economic Planning* (London, 1935), p. 32. The reader's attention is called to the first English translation of von Mises' work *Die Gemeinwirtschaft*, published under the title *Socialism* late in 1937. The translation, made by J. Kahane, is based on the revised 1932 edition of the German work.

The economist will scarcely find it possible to accept this claim. From the economist's point of view, he would have done better to confine himself to the formulation of the problem, as Pierson did; though, if he had done so, he probably would not have merited the great recognition of the socialists. For it was exactly Professor Mises' denial of the possibility of economic accounting under socialism that provided his challenge with such force and power. Thus the socialist and the economist will view the achievement of Professor Mises differently—a strange instance of the divergence of their opinions, which, as Professor Mises thinks, must be always the rule.

A solution of the problem, different from that advanced by Professor Mises, was suggested by Pareto as early as 1897[2] and was later elaborated by Barone.[3] The further discussion of the problem, with one exception, which will be mentioned later, has scarcely gone beyond what is already contained in Barone's paper.

Professor Mises' contention that a socialist economy cannot solve the problem of rational allocation of its resources is based on a confusion concerning the nature of prices. As Wicksteed has pointed out, the term "price" has two meanings. It may mean either price in the ordinary sense, i.e., the exchange ratio of two commodities on a market,

---

[2] Vilfredo Pareto, *Cours d'économie politique* (Lausanne, 1897), Vol. II, pp. 364ff. See also his *Manuel d'économie politique* (Paris, 1910), pp. 362–64.

[3] Enrico Barone, "Il ministerio della produzione nello stato collettivista," *Giornale degli Economisti,* 1908. This paper has also been published in English, under the title "The Ministry of Production in the Collectivist State," as an appendix to the volume on *Collectivist Economic Planning,* edited by Hayek.

or it may have the generalized meaning of "terms on which alternatives are offered." Wicksteed says, " 'Price,' then, in the narrower sense of 'the money for which a material thing, a service, or a privilege can be obtained,' is simply a special case of 'price' in the wider sense of 'the terms on which alternatives are offered to us.' "[4] It is only prices in the generalized sense which are indispensable to solving the problem of allocation of resources. The economic problem is a problem of *choice* between alternatives. To solve the problem three data are needed: (1) a preference scale which guides the acts of choice; (2) knowledge of the "terms on which alternatives are offered"; and (3) knowledge of the amount of resources available. Those three data being given, the problem of choice is soluble.

Now it is obvious that a socialist economy may regard the data under 1 and 3 as given, at least in as great a degree as they are given in a capitalist economy. The data under 1 may either be given by the demand schedules of the individuals or be established by the judgment of the authorities administering the economic system. The question remains whether the data under 2 are accessible to the administrators of a socialist economy. Professor Mises denies this. However, a careful study of price theory and of the theory of production convinces us that, the data

[4] P. H. Wicksteed, *The Common Sense of Political Economy* (2d ed., London, 1933), p. 28. Similarly Schumpeter has stated that the term "exchange ratio" may be used in a wider sense to indicate the alternatives available, so that production may be regarded as an "exchange" *sui generis*. Joseph Schumpeter, *Das Wesen und der Hauptinhalt der theoretischen Nationalökonomie* (Leipzig, 1908), pp. 50ff.

under 1 and under 3 being given, the "terms on which alternatives are offered" are determined ultimately by the technical possibilities of transformation of one commodity into another, i.e., by the production functions. The administrators of a socialist economy will have exactly the same knowledge, or lack of knowledge, of the production functions as the capitalist entrepreneurs have.

But Professor Mises seems to have confused prices in the narrower sense, i.e., the exchange ratios of commodities on a market, with prices in the wider sense of "terms on which alternatives are offered." As, in consequence of public ownership of the means of production, there is in a socialist economy no market on which capital goods are actually exchanged, there are obviously no prices of capital goods in the sense of exchange ratios on a market. And, hence, Professor Mises argues, there is no "index of alternatives" available in the sphere of capital goods. But this conclusion is based on a confusion of "price" in the narrower sense with "price" in the wider sense of an index of alternatives. It is only in the latter sense that "prices" are indispensable for the allocation of resources, and on the basis of the technical possibilities of transformation of one commodity into another they are also given in a socialist economy.

Professor Mises argues that private ownership of the means of production is indispensable for a rational allocation of resources. Since, according to him, without private ownership of the means of production no determinate index of alternatives exists (at least in the sphere of capital goods), the economic principles of choice between different alternatives are applicable only to a special institutional set-up, i.e., to a society which recognizes private ownership of the means of production. It has been maintained, indeed, by Marx[5] and by the historical school (in so far as the latter recognized any economic laws at all) that all economic laws have only historico-relative validity. But it is most surprising to find this institutionalist view supported by a prominent member of the Austrian school,[6] which did so much to emphasize the universal validity of the fundamental principles of economic theory.

Thus Professor Mises' denial of the possibility of economic calculation in a socialist system must be rejected. However, Professor Mises' argument has been taken up recently in a more refined form by Professor Hayek and Professor Robbins. They do not deny the *theoretical* possibility of a rational allocation of resources in a socialist economy; they only doubt the possibility of a satisfactory *practical* solution of the problem. Discussing the solution offered by Barone, Dickinson, and others, Professor Hayek says that "it must be admitted that this is not an impossi-

[5] With regard to Marx this statement requires certain qualifications. See the Appendix.

[6] I am, of course, perfectly aware that Professor Mises does not regard himself as an institutionalist and that he has stated explicitly the universal validity of economic theory (see *Grundprobleme der Nationalökonomie*, Jena, 1933, pp. 27–28). But there is a spectacular contradiction between this statement and his assertion that private ownership of the means of production is indispensable for a rational allocation of resources. For if this assertion is true, economics as the theory of allocation of resources is applicable only to a society with private ownership of the means of production. The implications of the denial of the possibility of rational choice in a socialist economy are plainly institutionalist.

bility in the sense that it is logically contradictory."[7] But he denies that the problem is capable of a practical solution in a society without private ownership of the means of production.[8]

The issue has been put very clearly by Professor Robbins. "On paper," he says, "we can conceive this problem to be solved by a series of mathematical calculations. . . . But in practice this solution is quite unworkable. It would necessitate the drawing up of millions of equations on the basis of millions of statistical data based on many more millions of individual computations. By the time the equations were solved, the information on which they were based would have become obsolete and they would need to be calculated anew. The suggestion that a practical solution of the problem of planning is possible on the basis of the Paretian equations simply indicates that those who put it forward have not grasped what these equations mean."[9]

Thus Professor Hayek and Professor Robbins have given up the essential point of Professor Mises' position and retreated to a second line of defense. In principle, they admit, the problem is soluble, but it is to be doubted whether in a socialist community it can be solved by a simple method of *trial and error,* as it is solved in the capitalist economy. The significance of the private ownership of the means of production and of an actual market

---

[7] "The Present State of the Debate," *Collectivist Economic Planning,* p. 207.
[8] *Ibid.,* pp. 208ff.
[9] L. C. Robbins, *The Great Depression* (London, 1934), p. 151.

for capital goods has shifted. Theoretically prices in the generalized sense of "terms on which alternatives are offered" are admitted to be given also without an actual market. The function of the market is, according to them, a different one, namely, to provide a method of allocating resources by trial and error. And it is this function a socialist economy would be deprived of.

The position taken by Professor Hayek and by Professor Robbins is a significant step forward in the discussion of the problem. It promises a much more fruitful approach than Professor Mises' wholesale denial of the possibility of economic accounting under socialism. Whether by having taken this step they, too, will merit an honorable statue, or at least a memorial tablet, in the building of the Ministry of Socialization or of the Central Planning Board is yet to be seen. The great importance of the problem makes it quite possible.

Barone has already pointed to the fact that the equations of economic equilibrium must be solved also in a socialist society by trial and error.[10] He regarded such a solution as possible but failed to indicate how it would be achieved. However, the way in which a socialist economy would solve the problem by a method of trial and error has been indicated quite clearly by Fred M. Taylor in a paper published in 1929.[11] This paper provides in substance the

[10] See "The Ministry of Production in the Collectivist State," *Collectivist Economic Planning*, pp. 286–89.

[11] "The Guidance of Production in a Socialist State," *American Economic Review*, March, 1929. Reprinted above on pages 41–54.

answer to Professor Hayek's and Professor Robbins' argument, and it is the first contribution which really goes beyond what is contained in Barone's paper. But the great importance of the argument of Hayek and Robbins necessitates a more detailed investigation of the problem. It is, therefore, the purpose of the present essay to elucidate the way in which the allocation of resources is effected by trial and error on a competitive market and to find out whether a similar trial and error procedure is not possible in a socialist economy.

II. The Determination of Equilibrium on a Competitive Market

Let us see how economic equilibrium is established by trial and error on a competitive market. By a competitive market we mean a market in which (1) the number of individuals is so great that no one of them can influence prices appreciably by varying his demand or supply and, therefore, is forced to regard prices as constant parameters independent of his behavior; (2) there is free entry into and exodus from each trade or industry.

The conditions of equilibrium are twofold: (A) All individuals participating in the economic system must attain their maximum positions on the basis of equilibrium prices; and (B) the equilibrium prices are determined by the condition that the demand for each commodity is equal to its supply. We may call the first the *subjective,* and the latter the *objective,* condition. These two conditions, however, do not determine equilibrium unless there is added a third condition which expresses *the social organization of the economic system.* In our case this condition states that: (C) the incomes of the consumers are equal to their receipts from selling the services of the productive resources they own, plus entrepreneurs' profits (which are zero in equilibrium).[12] This condition is no equilibrium condition in the strict sense, for it holds independently of whether the economic system is in equilibrium or not.[13] Notwithstanding, it is necessary to make equilibrium determinate. Let us analyze these three conditions, A, B, and C; A and B being the equilibrium conditions *sensu stricto.*

A. The subjective condition of equilibrium is carried out by the individuals'[14] maximizing their utility, profit, or income from the ownership of productive resources.

1. The consumers maximize the total utility they derive from their income by spending it so that the marginal utility of the amount obtainable for a unit of income (expressed in money) is equal for all commodities. Their incomes and the prices being given (the latter are necessary to determine what is the amount of a commodity obtainable for a unit of income), the demand for consumers' goods is determined.

[12] Such profits as do not vanish in equilibrium, because of entrepreneurial ability being a scarce factor of production, may be conveniently regarded as receipts from selling productive resources (i.e., entrepreneurial abilities).

[13] To put it in mathematical terms: this condition is an identity and not an equation.

[14] The term "individual" is used here in the broad connotation of *Wirtschaftssubjekt* so as to include also collective units (i.e., family households and joint-stock companies).

2. The producers maximize their profit. The process of maximizing profit is composed of two parts: (a) the determination of the optimum combination of factors and (b) the determination of the optimum scale of output. The first is attained by combining the factors of production in such proportion as to equalize the marginal productivity of the amount of each factor which can be purchased for a unit of money.[15] The prices of the factors being given, so that it is possible to determine what is the amount of each factor obtainable for a unit of money, this condition determines the minimum cost curve of the producer. This curve being given, the optimum scale of output is attained when the marginal cost is equal to the price of the product (which is given on the market). Thus the output of the single producer and his demand for factors of production are determined. This determination is based entirely on the first property of the competitive market, namely, that

[15] This statement has to be corrected if limitational factors are used in production. There are two kinds of limitational factors, according to whether the amount of the limitational factor which must be used in production is a function of the quantity of product we wish to obtain, or of the amount of another factor used. If limitational factors of the first kind are used the statement in the text holds for the substitutional factors, the amount of limitational factors necessary being determined by the scale of output chosen. If limitational factors of the second kind are used the marginal productivity of the substitutional factors must be proportional to their prices *plus* the marginal expenditure for the limitational factors which are a function of the substitutional factor in question; the amount of the limitational factors necessary is then determined by the amount of the substitutional factors used. As to limitational factors of the first kind, see N. Georgescu-Roegen, "Fixed Coefficient of Production and the Marginal Productivity Theory," *Review of Economic Studies,* Vol. III, No. 1, pp. 40–49 (October, 1935). Dr. Tord Palander has drawn my attention to the existence of the second kind of limitational factors.

the prices of the product and of the factors are independent of the scale of output and of the combination of factors chosen by the producer (because of the large number of competing producers). The determination of the total output of an industry is based on the other property of the competitive market, i.e., on the free entry of producers into, or their exodus from, any industry. This makes the total output of an industry such that the price of the product is equal to the average cost[16] of production. The output and demand for factors of production by each producer and the total output of an industry being given, the total demand for factors by an industry is determined, too. Thus, the prices of the products and of the factors being given, the supply of products and the demand for factors are determined.

3. The owners of the ultimate productive resources (labor, capital, and natural resources) maximize their income by selling the services of these resources to the highest bidder. The prices of the services of these resources being given, their distribution between the different industries is determined.[17]

B. The subjective condition of equilibrium can be carried out only on the basis of a *given* set of prices and of consumers' incomes. The prices are regarded by the individuals as constants independent of their behavior. For

[16] As used throughout this paper, average cost means average cost per unit of output.

[17] In order to simplify the exposition we disregard the fact that the amount of the resources available, instead of being constant, may depend on their price. Thus the total supply of labor may be a function of the wage rate. As to capital,

each set of prices and of consumers' incomes we get different quantities of commodities demanded and supplied. Condition C states that the incomes of the consumers are equal to their receipts from selling the services of the ultimate productive resources they own, plus entrepreneurs' profits. In virtue of this condition incomes of consumers are determined by prices of the services of ultimate productive resources and by profits so that, finally, prices alone remain as the variables determining demand and supply of commodities. By assuming different sets of prices we obtain the demand and supply schedules. Now, the objective condition of equilibrium serves to pick out a special set of prices as the only one which assures the compatibility of the subjective maximum positions of all individuals participating in the economic system. This condition means that the demand and the supply of each commodity have to be equal. Prices which satisfy this condition are the equilibrium prices. If the demand and supply schedules are all monotonic functions there exists only one set of prices which satisfies the objective equilibrium condition; otherwise, there may be a multiple solu-

its amount may be regarded in the short period as constant, whereas in the long run the rate of interest certainly affects saving. In long-period equilibrium the amount of capital is determined by the condition that the rate of its marginal *net* productivity is equal to the interest rate and to the time preference of the individuals (which may be, and probably is, zero). See the author's papers, "The Place of Interest in the Theory of Production," *Review of Economic Studies,* June, 1936, pp. 159–92, and "Professor Knight's Note on Interest Theory," *Review of Economic Studies,* June, 1937; also F. H. Knight, "Professor Fisher's Interest Theory," *Journal of Political Economy,* 39:197ff. (April, 1931); and Hayek, "Utility Analysis and Interest," *Economic Journal,* March, 1936, pp. 58–60.

tion, but some of the price sets obtained represent unstable equilibria.[18]

Such is the theoretical solution of the problem of equilibrium on a competitive market. Now let us see how the problem is solved actually by *trial and error*. The solution by trial and error is based on what may be called the *parametric function of prices,* i.e., on the fact that, although the prices are a resultant of the behavior of all individuals on the market, each individual separately regards the actual market prices as given data to which he has to adjust himself. Each individual tries to exploit the market situation confronting him which he cannot control. Market prices are thus parameters determining the behavior of the individuals. The equilibrium value of these parameters is determined by the objective equilibrium condition (B). As Walras has so brilliantly shown,[19] this is done by a series of successive trials *(tâtonnements)*.

Let us start with a set of prices given *at random* (for instance, by drawing numbers from an urn). On the basis of this *random* set of prices (Walras' *prix criés par hasard*) the individuals fulfill their subjective equilibrium condi-

[18] If the demand and supply schedules are not monotonic functions the first must have an increasing, and the latter must have a decreasing, branch. Demand can be an increasing function of price in the case of competing commodities and, as Walras has shown, supply can be a decreasing function of price when the commodity in question has a personal utility for the seller. If either demand is an increasing, or supply is a decreasing, function of price there may be a multiple solution even if those functions are monotonic. However, these are quite exceptional cases.

[19] Léon Walras, *Elements d'économie politique pure* (éd. définitive, Paris, 1926), pp. 65, 132-33, 214-15, 217ff., 259-60, 261ff.

tion and attain their maximum positions. For each commodity a quantity demanded and a quantity supplied is established. Now the objective equilibrium condition comes into play. If the quantity demanded and the quantity supplied of each commodity happen to be equal, the entire situation is settled and the prices are the equilibrium prices. If, however, the quantities demanded and the quantities supplied diverge, the competition of the buyers and sellers will alter the prices. Prices of those commodities the demand for which exceeds the supply rise, while the prices of the commodities where the reverse is the case fall. As a result we get a *new* set of prices, which serves as a new basis for the individuals' striving to satisfy their subjective equilibrium condition. The subjective equilibrium condition being carried out, we get a new set of quantities demanded and supplied. If demand and supply are not equal for each commodity, prices change again and we have *another* set of prices, which again serves as a basis for individual rearranging of choices; and thus we get a new set of quantities demanded and supplied. And so the process goes on until the objective equilibrium condition is satisfied and equilibrium finally reached.[20] Actually it is the *his-*

[20] Thus each successive set of prices is nearer to satisfying the objective equilibrium condition than the preceding one. However, since a change of the quantity supplied generally requires a period of time, some qualification must be made. In industries where changes of output can be effected in a more or less continuous way, by varying some factors of production and leaving the others unchanged, and by extending, as time goes on, the number of factors which are made variable, the process of adaptation is determined by a family of short-period supply (and cost) curves. With this type of adaptation, which may be termed Marshallian, each successive price is nearer to the equilibrium price. But

torically given prices which serve as a basis for the process of successive trials.

We have to apologize to the reader for having occupied his attention with this textbook exposition of the elements of the theory of economic equilibrium. But the very fact that the possibility of determining prices (in the wider sense of "terms on which alternatives are offered") in a socialist economy has been denied seems to indicate that the meaning of these elements has not been fully grasped. Now let us see whether a similar method of trial and error cannot be applied in a socialist economy.

III. THE TRIAL AND ERROR PROCEDURE IN A SOCIALIST ECONOMY

In order to discuss the method of allocating resources in a socialist economy we have to state what kind of socialist society we have in mind. The fact of public ownership of the means of production does not in itself determine the system of distributing consumers' goods and of allocating people to various occupations, nor the principles guiding the production of commodities. Let us now assume that freedom of choice in consumption and freedom of choice of occupation are maintained and that the preferences of consumers, as expressed by their demand prices, are the

where output can be varied only by jerks, as in the case of crops, the mechanism described by the cobweb theorem comes into action and successive trials approach equilibrium only under special conditions. However, the Marshallian type of adaptation of supply seems to be the dominant one. On this point see the author's paper "Formen der Angebotsanpassung und wirtschaftliches Gleichgewicht," *Zeitschrift für Nationalökonomie*, Bd. VI, Heft 3, 1935.

guiding criteria in production and in the allocation of resources. Later we shall pass to the study of a more centralized socialist system.[21]

In the socialist system as described we have a genuine market (in the institutional sense of the word) for consumers' goods and for the services of labor. But there is no market for capital goods and productive resources outside of labor.[22] The prices of capital goods and productive resources outside of labor are thus prices in the generalized sense, i.e., mere indices of alternatives available, fixed for accounting purposes. Let us see how economic equilibrium is determined in such a system. Just as in a competitive individualist regime, the determination of equilibrium consists of two parts. (A) On the basis of *given* indices of alternatives (which are market prices in the case of consumers' goods and the services of labor and accounting prices in all other cases) both the individuals participating in the economic system as consumers and as owners of the services of labor and the managers of production and of the ultimate resources outside of labor (i.e., of capital and

[21] In pre-war literature the terms socialism and collectivism were used to designate a socialist system as described above and the word communism was used to denote more centralized systems. The classical definition of socialism (and of collectivism) was that of a system which socializes production alone, while communism was defined as socializing both production and consumption. At the present time these words have become political terms with special connotations.

[22] To simplify the problem we assume that all means of production are public property. Needless to say, in any actual socialist community there must be a large number of means of production privately owned (e.g., by farmers, artisans, and small-scale entrepreneurs). But this does not introduce any new theoretical problem.

of natural resources) make decisions according to certain principles. These managers are assumed to be public officials. (B) The prices (whether market or accounting) are determined by the condition that the quantity of each commodity demanded is equal to the quantity supplied. The conditions determining the decisions under A form the *subjective,* while that under B is the *objective,* equilibrium condition. Finally, we have also a condition C, expressing the social organization of the economic system. As the productive resources outside of labor are public property, the incomes of the consumers are divorced from the ownership of those resources and the form of condition C (social organization) is determined by the *principles of income formation adopted.*

The possibility of determining condition C in different ways gives to a socialist society considerable freedom in matters of distribution of income. But the necessity of maintaining freedom in the choice of occupation limits the arbitrary use of this freedom, for there must be some connection between the income of a consumer and the services of labor performed by him. It seems, therefore, convenient to regard the income of consumers as composed of two parts: one part being the receipts for the labor services performed and the other part being a social dividend constituting the individual's share in the income derived from the capital and the natural resources owned by society. We assume that the distribution of the social dividend is based on certain principles, reserving the content of those principles for later discussion. Thus condition C is determinate and determines the incomes of the consumers in terms of prices of the services of labor and social dividend, which, in turn, may be regarded as determined by the total yield of capital and of the natural resources and by the principles adopted in distributing this yield.[23]

A. Let us consider the subjective equilibrium condition in a socialist economy:

1. Freedom of choice in consumption being assumed,[24] this part of the subjective equilibrium condition of a competitive market applies also to the market for consumers' goods in a socialist economy. The incomes of the consumers and the prices of consumers' goods being given, the demand for consumers' goods is determined.

2. The decisions of the managers of production are no longer guided by the aim of maximizing profit. Instead, certain rules are imposed on them by the Central Planning Board which aim at satisfying consumers' preferences in the best way possible. These rules determine the combination of factors of production and the scale of output.

One rule must impose the choice of the combination of factors which minimizes the average cost of production.

[23] In formulating condition C capital accumulation has to be taken into account. Capital accumulation may be done either "corporately" by deducting a certain part of the national income before the social dividend is distributed, or it may be left to the savings of individuals, or both methods may be combined. But "corporate" accumulation must certainly be the dominant form of capital formation in a socialist economy.

[24] Of course there may be also a sector of socialized consumption the cost of which is met by taxation. Such a sector exists also in capitalist society and comprises the provision not only of collective wants, in Cassel's sense, but also

This rule leads to the factors being combined in such proportion that the marginal productivity of that amount of each factor which is worth a unit of money is the same for all factors.[25] This rule is addressed to whoever makes decisions involving the problem of the optimum combination of factors, i.e., to managers responsible for running existing plants and to those engaged in building new plants. A second rule determines the scale of output by stating that output has to be fixed so that marginal cost is equal to the price of the product. This rule is addressed to two kinds of persons. First of all, it is addressed to the managers of plants and thus determines the scale of output of each plant and, together with the first rule, its demand for factors of production. The first rule, to whomever addressed, and the second rule when addressed to the managers of plants perform the same function that in a competitive system is carried out by the private producer's aiming to maximize his profit, when the prices of factors and of the product are independent of the amount of each factor used by him and of his scale of output.

The total output of an industry has yet to be determined. This is done by addressing the second rule also to the managers of a whole industry (e.g., to the directors of the National Coal Trust) as a principle to guide them in deciding whether an industry ought to be expanded (by

of other wants whose social importance is too great to be left to the free choice of individuals (for instance, free hospital service and free education). But this problem does not represent any theoretical difficulty and we may disregard it.

[25] See, however, the correction for limitational factors in footnote 15, page 67.

building new plants or enlarging old ones) or contracted (by not replacing plants which are wearing out). Thus each industry has to produce exactly as much of a commodity as can be sold or "accounted for" to other industries at a price which equals the marginal cost incurred *by the industry* in producing this amount. The marginal cost incurred by an industry is the cost to that industry (not to a particular plant) of doing whatever is necessary to produce an additional unit of output, the optimum combination of factors being used. This may include the cost of building new plants or enlarging old ones.[26]

Addressed to the managers of an industry, the second rule performs the function which under free competition is carried out by the free entry of firms into an industry or their exodus from it: i.e., it determines the output of an industry.[27] The second rule, however, has to be carried out irrespective of whether average cost is covered or not, even if it should involve plants or whole industries in losses.

Both rules can be put in the form of the simple request

[26] Since in practice such marginal cost is not a continuous function of output we have to compare the cost of each additional *indivisible input* with the receipts expected from the additional output thus secured. For instance, in a railway system as long as there are unused carriages the cost of putting them into use has to be compared with the additional receipts which may be obtained by doing so. When all the carriages available are used up to capacity, the cost of building and running additional carriages (and locomotives) has to be compared with the additional receipts expected to arise from such action. Finally, the question of building new tracks is decided upon the same principle. Cf. A. P. Lerner, "Statics and Dynamics in Socialist Economics," *Economic Journal*, 47:263–67 (June, 1937).

[27] The result, however, of following this rule coincides with the result obtained under free competition only in the case of constant returns to the industry (i.e., a homogeneous production function of the first degree). In this case

to use always the method of production (i.e., combination of factors) which minimizes average cost and to produce as much of each service or commodity as will equalize marginal cost and the price of the product, this request being addressed to whoever is responsible for the particular decision to be taken. Thus the output of each plant and industry and the total demand for factors of production by each industry are determined. To enable the managers of production to follow these rules the prices of the factors and of the products must, of course, be given. In the case of consumers' goods and services of labor they are determined on a market; in all other cases they are fixed by the Central Planning Board. Those prices being given, the supply of products and the demand for factors are determined.

The reasons for adopting the two rules mentioned are obvious. Since prices are indices of terms on which alternatives are offered, that method of production which will minimize average cost will also minimize the alternatives sacrificed. Thus the first rule means simply that each commodity must be produced with a minimum sacrifice of

marginal cost incurred by the industry equals average cost. In all other cases the results diverge, for under free competition the output of an industry is such that average cost equals the price of the product, while according to our rule it is marginal cost (incurred by the industry) that ought to be equal to the price. This difference results in profits being made by the industries whose marginal cost exceeds average cost, whereas the industries in which the opposite is the case incur losses. These profits and losses correspond to the taxes and bounties proposed by Professor Pigou in order to bring about under free competition the equality of private and social marginal net product. See A. C. Pigou, *The Economics of Welfare* (3d ed., London, 1929), pp. 223–27.

alternatives. The second rule is a necessary consequence of following consumers' preferences. It means that the marginal significance of each preference which is satisfied has to be equal to the marginal significance of the alternative preferences the satisfaction of which is sacrificed. If the second rule was not observed certain lower preferences would be satisfied while preferences higher up on the scale would be left unsatisfied.

3. Freedom of choice of occupation being assumed, laborers offer their services to the industry or occupation paying the highest wages. For the publicly owned capital and natural resources a price has to be fixed by the Central Planning Board with the provision that these resources can be directed only to industries which are able to "pay," or rather to "account for," this price. This is a consequence of following the consumers' preferences. The prices of the services of the ultimate productive resources being given, their distribution between the different industries is also determined.

B. The subjective equilibrium condition can be carried out only when prices are *given*. This is also true of the decisions of the managers of production and of the productive resources in public ownership. Only when prices are given can the combination of factors which minimizes average cost, the output which equalizes marginal cost and the price of the product, and the best allocation of the ultimate productive resources be determined. But if there is no market (in the institutional sense of the word) for capital goods or for the ultimate productive resources outside of labor, can their prices be determined objectively? Must not the prices fixed by the Central Planning Board necessarily be quite arbitrary? If so, their arbitrary character would deprive them of any economic significance as indices of the terms on which alternatives are offered. This is, indeed, the opinion of Professor Mises.[28] And the view is shared by Mr. Cole, who says: "A planless economy, in which each entrepreneur takes his decisions apart from the rest, obviously confronts each entrepreneur with a broadly given structure of costs, represented by the current level of wages, rent, and interest. . . . In a planned socialist economy there can be no objective structure of costs. Costs can be imputed to any desired extent. . . . But these imputed costs are not objective, but *fiat* costs determined by the public policy of the State."[29] This view, however, is easily refuted by recalling the very elements of price theory.

Why is there an objective price structure in a competitive market? Because, as a result of the parametric function of prices, there is generally only *one* set of prices which satisfies the objective equilibrium condition, i.e., equalizes demand and supply of each commodity. The same objective price structure can be obtained in a socialist economy if the *parametric function of prices* is retained. On a competitive market the parametric function of prices results from the number of competing individuals being too large

---

[28] "Economic Calculation in the Socialist Commonwealth," reprinted in *Collectivist Economic Planning,* p. 112.

[29] G. D. H. Cole, *Economic Planning* (New York, 1935), pp. 183–84.

to enable any one to influence prices by his own action. In a socialist economy, production and ownership of the productive resources outside of labor being centralized, the managers certainly can and do influence prices by their decisions. Therefore, the parametric function of prices must be imposed on them by the Central Planning Board as an *accounting rule*. All accounting has to be done *as if* prices were independent of the decisions taken. For purposes of accounting, prices must be treated as constant, as they are treated by entrepreneurs on a competitive market.

The technique of attaining this end is very simple: the Central Planning Board has to fix prices and see to it that all managers of plants, industries, and resources do their accounting on the basis of the prices fixed by the Central Planning Board, and not tolerate any use of other accounting. Once the parametric function of prices is adopted as an accounting rule, the price structure is established by the objective equilibrium condition. For each set of prices and consumers' incomes a definite amount of each commodity is supplied and demanded. Condition C determines the incomes of the consumers by the prices of the services of ultimate productive resources and the principles adopted for the distribution of the social dividend. With those principles given, prices alone are the variables determining the demand and supply of commodities.

The condition that the quantity demanded and supplied has to be equal for each commodity serves to select the equilibrium prices which alone assure the compatibility of all decisions taken. *Any price different from the equilibrium price would show at the end of the accounting period a surplus or a shortage of the commodity in question.* Thus the accounting prices in a socialist economy, far from being arbitrary, have quite the same objective character as the market prices in a regime of competition. Any mistake made by the Central Planning Board in fixing prices would announce itself in a very objective way—by a physical shortage or surplus of the quantity of the commodity or resources in question—and would have to be corrected in order to keep production running smoothly. As there is generally only one set of prices which satisfies the objective equilibrium condition, both the prices of products and costs[30] are uniquely determined.[31]

Our study of the determination of equilibrium prices in a socialist economy has shown that the process of price determination is quite analogous to that in a competitive market. The Central Planning Board performs the func-

[30] Hayek maintains that it would be impossible to determine the value of durable instruments of production because, in consequence of changes, "the value of most of the more durable instruments of production has little or no connection with the costs which have been incurred in their production" (*Collectivist Economic Planning,* p. 227). It is quite true that the value of such durable instruments is essentially a capitalized quasi-rent and therefore can be determined only after the price which will be obtained for the product is known (cf. *ibid.,* p. 228). But there is no reason why the price of the product should be any less determinate in a socialist economy than on a competitive market. The managers of the industrial plant in question have simply to take the price fixed by the Central Planning Board as the basis of their calculation. The Central Planning Board would fix this price so as to satisfy the objective equilibrium condition, just as a competitive market does.

[31] However, in certain cases there may be a multiple solution. Cf. p. 69 above.

tions of the market. It establishes the rules for combining factors of production and choosing the scale of output of a plant, for determining the output of an industry, for the allocation of resources, and for the parametric use of prices in accounting. Finally, it fixes the prices so as to balance the quantity supplied and demanded of each commodity. It follows that a substitution of planning for the functions of the market is quite possible and workable.

Two problems deserve some special attention. The first relates to the determination of the best distribution of the social dividend. Freedom of choice of occupation assumed, the distribution of the social dividend may affect the amount of services of labor offered to different industries. If certain occupations received a larger social dividend than others, labor would be diverted into the occupations receiving a larger dividend. Therefore, the distribution of the social dividend must be such as not to interfere with the optimum distribution of labor services between the different industries and occupations. The optimum distribution is that which makes the differences of the value of the marginal product of the services of labor in different industries and occupations equal to the differences in the marginal disutility[32] of working in those industries or

---

[32] It is only the *relative* disutility of different occupations that counts. The absolute disutility may be zero or even negative. By putting leisure, safety, agreeableness of work, etc., into the preference scales, all labor costs may be expressed as opportunity costs. If such a device is adopted each industry or occupation may be regarded as producing a joint product: the commodity or service in question *and* leisure, safety, agreeableness of work, etc. The services of labor have to be allocated so that the value of this marginal *joint* product is the same in all industries and occupations.

occupations.[33] This distribution of the services of labor arises automatically whenever wages are the only source of income. *Therefore, the social dividend must be distributed so as to have no influence whatever on the choice of occupation.* The social dividend paid to an individual must be entirely independent of his choice of occupation. For instance, it can be divided equally per head of population, or distributed according to age or size of family or any other principle which does not affect the choice of occupation.

The other problem is the determination of the rate of interest. We have to distinguish between a short-period and a long-period solution of the problem. For the former the amount of capital is regarded as constant, and the rate of interest is simply determined by the condition that the demand for capital is equal to the amount available. When the rate of interest is set too low the socialized banking system would be unable to meet the demand of industries for capital; when the interest rate is set too high there would be a surplus of capital available for investment. However, in the long period the amount of capital can be increased by accumulation. If the accumulation of capital is performed "corporately" before distributing the social dividend to the individuals, the rate of accumulation can

[33] If the total amount of labor performed is not limited by legislation or custom regulating the hours of work, etc., the value of the marginal product of the services of labor in each occupation has to be *equal* to the marginal disutility. If any limitational factors are used, it is the marginal *net* product of the services of labor (obtained by deducting from the marginal product the marginal expenditure for the limitational factors) which has to satisfy the condition in the text.

be determined by the Central Planning Board *arbitrarily*. The Central Planning Board will probably aim at accumulating enough to make the marginal *net* productivity of capital zero,[34] this aim being never attained because of technical progress (new labor-saving devices), increase of population, the discovery of new natural resources, and, possibly, because of the shift of demand toward commodities produced by more capital-intensive methods.[35] But the rate, i.e., the *speed,* at which accumulation progresses is arbitrary.

The arbitrariness of the rate of capital accumulation "corporately" performed means simply that the decision regarding the rate of accumulation reflects how the Central Planning Board, and not the consumers, evaluate the optimum time-shape of the income stream. One may argue, of course, that this involves a diminution of consumers' welfare. This difficulty could be overcome only by leaving all accumulation to the saving of individuals.[36] But this is scarcely compatible with the organization of a socialist society.[37] Discussion of this point is postponed to a later part of this essay.

[34] Cf. Knut Wicksell, "Professor Cassel's System of Economics," reprinted in his *Lectures on Political Economy* (L. Robbins, ed., 2 vols., London, 1934), Vol. I, p. 241.

[35] These changes, however, if very frequent, may act also in the opposite direction and diminish the marginal *net* productivity of capital because of the risk of obsolescence due to them. This is pointed out by A. P. Lerner in "A Note on Socialist Economics," *Review of Economic Studies,* October, 1936, p. 72.

[36] This method has been advocated by Barone in "The Ministry of Production in the Collectivist State," *Collectivist Economic Planning,* pp. 278–79.

[37] Of course, the consumers remain free to save as much as they want out of the income which is actually paid out to them, and the socialized banks could

Having treated the theoretical determination of economic equilibrium in a socialist society, let us see how equilibrium can be determined by a method of *trial and error* similar to that in a competitive market. This method of trial and error is based on the *parametric function of prices*. Let the Central Planning Board start with a given set of prices chosen *at random*. All decisions of the managers of production and of the productive resources in public ownership and also all decisions of individuals as consumers and as suppliers of labor are made on the basis of these prices. As a result of these decisions the quantity demanded and supplied of each commodity is determined. If the quantity demanded of a commodity is not equal to the quantity supplied, the price of that commodity has to be changed. It has to be raised if demand exceeds supply and lowered if the reverse is the case. Thus the Central Planning Board fixes a new set of prices which serves as a basis for new decisions, and which results in a new set of quantities demanded and supplied. Through this process of trial and error equilibrium prices are finally determined. Actually the process of trial and error would, of course, proceed on the basis of the prices *historically given*. Relatively small adjustments of those prices would constantly be made, and there would be no necessity of building up an entirely new price system.

pay interest on savings. As a matter of fact, in order to prevent hoarding they would have to do so. But *this* rate of interest would not have any necessary connection with the marginal *net* productivity of capital. It would be quite arbitrary.

This process of trial and error has been excellently described by the late Professor Fred M. Taylor. He assumes that the administrators of the socialist economy would assign provisional values to the factors of production (as well as to all other commodities). He continues:

If, in regulating productive processes, the authorities were actually using for any particular factor a valuation which was too high or too low, that fact would soon disclose itself in unmistakable ways. Thus, supposing that, in the case of a particular factor, the valuation . . . was too high, that fact would inevitably lead the authorities to be unduly economical in the use of that factor; and this conduct, in turn, would make the amount of that factor which was available for the current production period larger than the amount which was consumed during that period. In other words, too high a valuation of any factor would cause the stock of that factor to show a surplus at the end of the productive period.[38]

Similarly, too low a valuation would cause a deficit in the stock of that factor. "Surplus or deficit—one or the other of these would result from every wrong valuation of a factor."[39] By a set of successive trials the right accounting prices of the factors are found.

Thus the accounting prices in a socialist economy can be determined by the same process of trial and error by which prices on a competitive market are determined. To determine the prices the Central Planning Board does not need to have "complete lists of the different quantities of all commodities which would be bought at any possible combination of prices of the different commodities which might

[38] "The Guidance of Production in a Socialist State." See page 53 above.
[39] Ibid.

be available."[40] Neither would the Central Planning Board have to solve hundreds of thousands (as Professor Hayek expects[41]) or millions (as Professor Robbins thinks[42]) of equations. The only "equations" which would have to be "solved" would be those of the consumers and the managers of production. These are exactly the same "equations" which are "solved" in the present economic system and the persons who do the "solving" are the same also. Consumers "solve" them by spending their income so as to get out of it the maximum total utility; and the managers of production "solve" them by finding the combination of factors that minimizes average cost and the scale of output that equalizes marginal cost and the price of the product. They "solve" them by a method of trial and error, making (or imagining) small variations *at the margin,* as Marshall used to say, and watching what effect those variations have either on the total utility or on the cost of production. And only a few of them have been graduated in higher mathematics. Professor Hayek and Professor Robbins themselves "solve" at least hundreds of equations daily, for instance, in buying a newspaper or in deciding to take a meal in a restaurant, and presumably they do not use determinants or Jacobians for that purpose. And each entrepreneur who hires or discharges a worker, or who buys a bale of cotton, "solves equations" too. Exactly the same kind and number of "equations," no less and no more, have to be "solved" in a socialist as in a capitalist

[40] "The Present State of the Debate," *Collectivist Economic Planning,* p. 211.
[41] *Ibid.,* p. 212.   [42] *The Great Depression,* p. 151.

economy, and exactly the same persons, the consumers and managers of production plants, have to "solve" them.

To establish the prices which serve the persons "solving equations" as parameters no mathematics is needed either. Neither is there needed any knowledge of the demand and supply functions. The right prices are simply found out by watching the quantities demanded and the quantities supplied and by raising the price of a commodity or service whenever there is an excess of demand over supply and lowering it whenever the reverse is the case, until, by trial and error, the price is found at which demand and supply are in balance.

As we have seen, there is not the slightest reason why a trial and error procedure, similar to that in a competitive market, could not work in a socialist economy to determine the accounting prices of capital goods and of the productive resources in public ownership. Indeed, it seems that this trial and error procedure would, or at least could, work *much better* in a socialist economy than it does in a competitive market. For the Central Planning Board has a much wider knowledge of what is going on in the whole economic system than any private entrepreneur can ever have, and, consequently, may be able to reach the right equilibrium prices by a *much shorter* series of successive trials than a competitive market actually does.[43] The argu-

[43] In reducing the number of trials necessary a knowledge of the demand and supply schedules derived from statistics, on which Dickinson wants to base the pricing of goods in a socialist economy, may be of great service, but such knowledge, although *useful*, is *not necessary* in finding out the equilibrium

ment that in a socialist economy the accounting prices of capital goods and of productive resources in public ownership cannot be determined objectively, either because this is theoretically impossible, or because there is no adequate trial and error procedure available, cannot be maintained. In 1911 Professor Taussig classified the argument that "goods could not be valued" among the objections to socialism that are "of little weight."[44] After all the discussions since that time, no reason can be found to change this opinion.

IV. THE GENERAL APPLICABILITY OF THE TRIAL AND ERROR METHOD

The procedure of trial and error described is also applicable to a socialist system where freedom of choice in consumption and freedom of choice of occupation are nonexistent and where the allocation of resources, instead of being directed by the preferences of consumers, is directed by the aims and valuations of the bureaucracy in charge of the administration of the economic system. In such a

prices. However, if the Central Planning Board proceeds in fixing prices purely by trial and error and the managers of production adhere strictly to treating the prices fixed as constant, in certain branches of production the fluctuations described by the cobweb theorem might appear also in a socialist economy. In such cases the Planning Board would have, in order to avoid such fluctuations, deliberately to use anticipations as to the influence of variations of output on the price of the product, and vice versa (i.e., a knowledge of demand and supply schedules) in fixing the accounting prices. Such deliberate use of demand and supply schedules is useful in all other cases, too, for it serves to shorten the series of trials and thus avoids unnecessary waste.

[44] F. W. Taussig, *Principles of Economics* (New York, 1911), Vol. II, p. xvi. See also pp. 456–57.

system the Central Planning Board decides which commodities are to be produced and in what quantities, the consumers' goods produced being distributed to the citizens by rationing and the various occupations being filled by assignment. In such a system also rational economic accounting is possible, only that the accounting reflects the preferences of the bureaucrats in the Central Planning Board, instead of those of the consumers. The Central Planning Board has to fix a scale of preferences which serves as the basis of valuation of consumers' goods.

The construction of such a preference scale is by no means a practical impossibility. The consumer on a competitive market is never in doubt as what to choose if only the prices of the commodities are given, though he certainly would find it impossible to write down the mathematical formula of his utility (or rather preference) function. Similarly, the Central Planning Board does not need to have an elaborate formula of its preferences. By simple judgment it would assign, for instance, to a hat the valuation of ten monetary units when 100,000 hats are produced monthly, and a valuation of eight monetary units to a hat when 150,000 hats per month are produced.

The preference scale of the Central Planning Board being given, the prices, which in this case are *all* accounting prices, are determined in exactly the same way as before. The Central Planning Board has to impose on the managers and builders of plants the rule that factors of production should be combined so as to minimize the average cost of production. For each plant and each industry the rule must be adopted to produce exactly as much of a commodity as can be "accounted for" at a price equaling marginal cost; and on the managers of ultimate productive resources the rule must be imposed to direct these resources only to the industries which can "account for" the price fixed by the Central Planning Board. The last two rules were formerly consequences of following the preferences of the consumers, now they are consequences of keeping to the preference scale fixed by the Central Planning Board. They are thus rules which make the decisions of the managers of production and of productive resources consistent with the aims set by the Central Planning Board. In other words, they are rules of internal *consistency* of the planned economy. The rule to choose the combination of factors that minimizes average cost secures *efficiency* in carrying out the plan.

Finally, the Central Planning Board has to impose the parametric function of the accounting prices fixed by itself and to fix them so as to balance the quantity supplied and the quantity demanded for each commodity. The price fixing can be done by trial and error, exactly as in the case studied above; the equilibrium prices thus fixed have a definite objective meaning. The prices are "planned" in so far as the preference scale is fixed by the Central Planning Board; but once the scale is fixed, they are quite determinate. Any price different from the equilibrium price would leave at the end of the accounting period a surplus or a shortage of the commodity in question and thus impair the smooth running of the production process. The use of the right accounting prices is vital to avoid disturbances in the *physical* course of production and those prices are far from being arbitrary.

The determinateness of the accounting prices holds, however, only if all discrepancies between demand and supply of a commodity are met by an appropriate change of its price. Thus, outside of the distribution of consumers' goods to the citizens, rationing has to be excluded as a method of equalizing supply and demand. If rationing is used for this purpose the prices become arbitrary. But it is interesting to observe that, even if rationing is used, there is, within limits, a tendency to produce the same quantities of commodities as would have been produced if all adjustments between demand and supply were made exclusively by price fixing. If, for instance, the accounting price has been set too low, there is an excess of demand over supply. The Central Planning Board would have to interfere in such a case and order the industry producing the commodity in question to increase its output while ordering the industries using this commodity as a factor of production to be more economical in its use.[45]

[45]Let *DD'* and *SS'* be the demand and the supply curves respectively. *BQ* is the equilibrium price and *OB* the equilibrium quantity. If the price is set at *AP* the quantity *OA* is forthcoming while *OC* is demanded. As a result of the intervention of the Planning Board the quantity produced will be set somewhere between *OA* and *OC*.

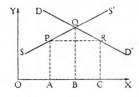

Thus the method of rationing leads, by a very rough approximation, to the point where fixing the equilibrium price would have led. But if rationing becomes a general procedure the rules enumerated above cease to be reliable indices of the consistency between the decisions of the managers of production and the aims established by the plan. The consistency of those decisions with the plan can be, instead, measured by fixing quotas of output and comparing them with the actual achievement (as is done in the Soviet Union). But there is no way of measuring the *efficiency* in carrying out the plan without a system of accounting prices which satisfies the objective equilibrium condition, for the rule to produce at the minimum average cost has no significance with regard to the aims of the plan unless prices represent the relative scarcity of the factors of production.[46]

[46] There exists, however, a special case where prices are not needed to carry out the plan efficiently. This is the case of constant coefficients of production. If all factors of production are limitational there is no economic problem in finding out the best combination of factors. The combination of factors of production is imposed by the technological exigencies of production. But there remains the problem of determining the optimum scale of output and for this purpose the prices of the factors of production are needed. But if the amount required of all factors of production is simply proportional either to the quantity of the product (if the limitational factors are of the first kind) or to the quantity of another factor used (if the limitational factors are of the second kind)—this is Pareto's case of constant coefficients of production—marginal cost is independent of the scale of output. The problem of choosing the optimum scale of output is thus ruled out too. In the particular case under consideration, where all coefficients of production are constant, no prices and no cost accounting whatever are needed. Efficiency in production is maintained merely by technological considerations of avoiding waste of materials, etc. It seems that those who deny the necessity of an adequate price system in a socialist economy have this case in mind. If the quotas of consumers' goods to be produced are given, all further

By demonstrating the economic consistency and workability of a socialist economy with free choice neither in consumption nor in occupation, but directed rather by a preference scale imposed by the bureaucrats in the Central Planning Board, we do not mean, of course, to recommend such a system. Mr. Lerner has sufficiently shown the undemocratic character of such a system and its incompatibility with the ideals of the socialist movement.[47] Such a system would scarcely be tolerated by any civilized people. A distribution of consumers' goods by rationing was possible in the Soviet Union at a time when the standard of living was at a physiological minimum and an increase of the ration of any food, clothing, or housing accommodation was welcome, no matter what it was. But as soon as the national income increased sufficiently, rationing was given up, to be replaced to a large extent by a market for consumers' goods. And, outside of certain exceptions, there has always been freedom of choice of occupation in the Soviet Union. A distribution of consumers' goods by rationing is quite unimaginable in the countries of Western Europe or in the United States.

But freedom of choice in consumption does not imply

problems of planning production are purely technological and no price system or cost accounting is needed. But we need not say how extremely unrealistic is the assumption that all coefficients of production are constant. The very fact that in the Soviet Union such great stress is laid on cost accounting shows how far from reality this special case is removed. But if cost accounting is to fulfill its purpose of securing efficiency in carrying out the plan, the accounting prices cannot be arbitrary.

[47] "Economic Theory and Socialist Economy," *Review of Economic Studies*, October, 1934, pp. 51–61.

that production is actually guided by the choices of the consumers. One may well imagine a system in which production and the allocation of resources are guided by a preference scale fixed by the Central Planning Board while the price system is used to distribute the consumers' goods produced. In such a system there is freedom of choice in consumption, but the consumers have no influence whatever on the decisions of the managers of production and of the productive resources.[48] There would be two sets of prices of consumers' goods. One would be the market prices at which the goods are sold to the consumers; the other, the accounting prices derived from the preference scale fixed by the Central Planning Board. The latter set of prices would be those on the basis of which the managers of production would make their decisions.

However, it does not seem very probable that such a system would be tolerated by the citizens of a socialist community. The dual system of prices of consumers' goods would reveal to the people that the bureaucrats in the Central Planning Board allocate the community's productive resources according to a preference scale different from that of the citizens. The existence of a dual price

[48] Of course, there remains the possibility of influence through political channels, but there is no regular economic mechanism through which the consumers automatically influence the direction of production. Zassenhaus has suggested a very interesting theoretical formulation of the influence through political channels, analogous to the economic theory of choice. See "Ueber die ökonomische Theorie der Planwirtschaft," *Zeitschrift für Nationalökonomie,* Bd. V, pp. 511ff. (September, 1934).

system of consumers' goods could scarcely be concealed from the people, especially if there existed an institution (like the Workers' and Peasants' Inspection in the Soviet Union[49]) giving to the rank and file citizen the right to pry into the bookkeeping and into the management of the community's resources.

Thus the accounting prices of consumers' goods would be permitted to deviate from the market prices only in exceptional cases in which there is general agreement that such deviation is in the interest of social welfare. For instance, it might be agreed upon that the consumption of whisky ought to be discouraged, while the reading of the works of Karl Marx or of the Bible (or of both, as certainly would be the case in an Anglo-Saxon community) ought to be encouraged, and the prices of those things would be fixed accordingly. But such things do happen also in a capitalist society. If the bureaucrats want successfully to impose a preference scale of their own for the guidance of production, they have to camouflage the inconsistency of their preference scale with that of the citizens by resorting to rationing in the sphere of producers' goods and of resources.[50] Thus a socialist community which has

[49] This institution was abolished in June, 1934, and replaced by the Commission of Soviet Control. A part of its functions has been taken over by the trade-unions. See Sidney and Beatrice Webb, *Soviet Communism* (London, 1935), Vol. I, pp. 99 and 474–78.

[50] It seems that the great extent to which rationing was used in the Soviet Union was partly due to the necessity of concealing the share of the national income going to the bureaucracy but mainly to the failure properly to understand and utilize the price mechanism. Its continuance after the civil war and reconstruction is a symptom of the bureaucratic degeneration of the Soviet economy.

been able to impose the principle that rationing must be excluded, and price fixing used as the only method of balancing quantities demanded and quantities supplied,[51] may be fairly confident that it will be able to ensure that the Central Planning Board follows the preferences of the consumers.

V. The Economist's Case for Socialism

The rules of consistency of decisions and of efficiency in carrying them out in a socialist economy are exactly the same as those that govern the actual behavior of entrepreneurs on a purely competitive market.[52] Competition forces entrepreneurs to act much as they would have to act were they managers of production in a socialist system. The fact that free competition tends to enforce rules of behavior similar to those in an ideal planned economy makes competition the pet idea of the economist. But if competition enforces the same rules of allocating resources as would have to be accepted in a rationally conducted

[51] It is possible to imagine a Supreme Economic Court whose function would be to safeguard the use of the nation's productive resources in accordance with the public interest. It would have the power to repeal decisions of the Central Planning Board that were in contradiction to the general rules of consistency and efficiency discussed above, just as the United States Supreme Court has the power to repeal laws held unconstitutional. This court would have to repeal any decisions involving rationing.

[52] There seems to exist an apparent exception: the rule which determines the output of an industry. Under free competition the output of an industry is such that the price of the product is equal to the average cost of production, while the social optimum output (i.e., the output which best satisfies consumers' preferences) is obtained when the output of an industry is such that the price of the product is equal to the *marginal* cost incurred by the industry in producing

socialist economy, what is the use of bothering about socialism? Why change the whole economic system if the same result can be attained within the present system, if only it could be forced to maintain the competitive standard?

But the analogy between the allocation of resources in a competitive capitalist and a socialist economy is only a purely formal one. The *formal* principles are the same, but the *actual* allocation may be quite different. This difference is due to two features[53] that distinguish a socialist economy from an economic system based on private ownership of the means of production and on private enterprise.

One feature is the distribution of incomes (condition C in the determination of economic equilibrium). Only a socialist economy can distribute incomes so as to attain the maximum social welfare. In any system with private ownership of the means of production, the distribution of incomes is determined by the distribution of ownership of the ultimate productive resources. This distribution is a

that amount. When the industry works under constant returns there is no difference, for average and marginal cost incurred by the industry are equal. If, however, external economies or diseconomies of scale are present, there is a divergence which has already been noted by Marshall and explicitly recognized by Professor Pigou. See Alfred Marshall, *Principles of Economics* (8th ed., London, 1930), pp. 472 and 474–75; also Pigou, *The Economics of Welfare*, pp. 223–25. But this exception can be interpreted as due to a difference in the comprehensiveness of the items that enter into the accounting of costs and benefits (discussed on page 105 below).

[53] These two features, though without reference to a socialist economy, have been touched upon already by Marshall in discussing the doctrine of maximum satisfaction. See *Principles of Economics*, pp. 470–72.

historical datum which originates independently of the requirements of the maximization of social welfare. For instance, the distribution of landed property is different in countries where the big landed estates of the feudal epoch have been broken up by bourgeois and peasant revolutions than where they have been left intact. Under capitalism the distribution of the ownership of the ultimate productive resources is a very unequal one, a large part of the population owning only their labor power. Under such conditions demand price does not reflect the relative urgency of the needs of different persons,[54] and the allocation of resources determined by the demand price offered for consumers' goods is far from attaining the maximum of social welfare. While some are starving others are allowed to indulge in luxury. In a socialist society the incomes of the consumers could be determined so as to maximize the total welfare of the whole population.

Free choice in consumption and free choice of occupation being assumed, the distribution of incomes maximizing the total welfare of society has to satisfy the following

[54] This criticism presupposes, of course, that the various utilities derived from a given income by different persons are comparable. The theory of economic equilibrium does not need any such assumption, for being an *explanation* of behavior under given conditions, it is concerned only with individuals, each maximizing his utility separately. But the possibility of such comparison is a postulate necessary (except in a Robinson Crusoe economy) if different equilibrium positions are to be interpreted in terms of *human welfare*. And such interpretation is required for choosing different economic *policies*. If this possibility is denied, any judgment as to the merits of economic policies, transcending the question of purely formal consistency of decisions and of efficiency in carrying them out, is impossible. In such case also no reason can be found why the allocation of resources ought to be based on the demand prices resulting from the

two conditions: (1) The distribution has to be such that the same demand price offered by different consumers represents an equal urgency of need. This is attained if the marginal utility of income is the same for all consumers. (2) The distribution has to lead to such apportionment of the services of labor between the different occupations as to make the differences of the value of the marginal product of labor in the various occupations equal to the differences in the marginal disutility involved in their pursuit.[55] Assuming the marginal utility curves of income to be the same for all individuals, condition 1 is satisfied when all consumers have the same income. But condition 2 requires a differentiation of incomes, since, to secure the apportionment of labor services required, differences in the marginal disutility of the various occupations have to be compensated by differences in incomes. The contradiction, however, is only apparent. By putting leisure, safety, agreeableness of work, etc., into the utility scales of the individuals, the disutility of any occupation can be represented as opportunity cost. The choice of an occupation offering a lower money income, but also a smaller disutility, may be

free consumers' choices, rather than on the whim of a dictator. Any other preference scale chosen at random by the Central Planning Board would do equally well. To deny the comparability of the urgency of need of different persons and at the same time to regard the allocation of resources based on demand prices as the only one consistent with economic principles would be contradictory. It would be, as Mr. Dobb has rightly observed, a maneuver which enables "the scientific dignity of an ethical neutrality to be combined with an undiminished capacity to deliver judgments on practical affairs." (M. H. Dobb, "Economic Theory and the Problem of a Socialist Economy," *Economic Journal*, December, 1933, p. 591.) The logical fallacy of such a trick is easily exposed.

[55] Compare, however, the qualification contained in footnote 33, page 84.

interpreted as the purchase of leisure, safety, agreeableness of work, etc., at a price equal to the difference between the money income earned in that particular occupation and in others. Thus the differences of incomes required by condition 2 are only apparent. They represent prices paid by the individuals for different conditions of work. Instead of attaching different money incomes to the various occupations, the administration of a socialist economy might pay all citizens the same money income and charge a price for the pursuit of each occupation. It becomes obvious not only that there is no contradiction between both conditions, but that condition 2 is necessary to satisfy condition 1.[56]

Our argument holds strictly if the marginal utility curve of income is the same for all individuals.[57] Of course, this does not correspond to reality, and one might think of

[56] Thus Mr. Dobb is wrong when he maintains that these conditions are contradictory. (See *op. cit.*, pp. 591–92.) Unless education and training for the different occupations are free, condition 1 is also necessary to satisfy condition 2, for if the marginal utility of income were not the same for all persons the value of the marginal product of the services of labor (which is equal to wages) would be higher, relative to the disutility, in those occupations which have a higher cost of training. This happens in capitalist society where those who can afford expensive education and training are paid out of any proportion to the relative disutility of their work. Condition 2 would not work, however, in the case of exceptional talents (for instance, of prominent artists or surgeons), which form a natural monopoly. In such cases the value of the marginal product of the services of labor must be necessarily out of any proportion to the marginal disutility. If rewarded according to the value of the marginal product of their services such persons would form a privileged group drawing very high incomes (e.g., writers in the Soviet Union). But a socialist society might also pay them incomes which are far below the value of the marginal product of their services without affecting the supply of those services.

[57] This does *not* imply that all individuals have the same utility scales, although it would follow from such an assumption.

taking into account the differences between the marginal utility curves of income of different individuals by granting higher incomes to the more "sensitive" persons. But since such differences as in "sensitiveness" cannot be measured the scheme would be impracticable. Besides, the differences in "sensitiveness" existing in present society are chiefly due to the social barriers between classes, e.g., a Hungarian count being more "sensitive" than a Hungarian peasant. Such differences would disappear in the relatively homogeneous social stratification of a socialist society, and all differences as to "sensitiveness" would be of purely individual character. Such individual differences may be assumed to be distributed according to the normal law of error.[58] Thus, basing the distribution of incomes on the assumption that all individuals have the same marginal utility curve of income, a socialist society would strike the right average in estimating the relative urgency of the needs of different persons, leaving only random errors, while the distribution of income in capitalist society introduces a constant error—a class bias in favor of the rich.

The other feature which distinguishes a socialist economy from one based on private enterprise is the *comprehensiveness* of the items entering into the price system. What enters into the price system depends on the historically given set of institutions. As Professor Pigou has shown, there is frequently a divergence between the private cost borne by

---

[58] Such differences in the marginal utility curves of income of different individuals as are not purely random but due to age, family status, infirmity, etc., would be easily recognized, and incomes could be differentiated accordingly.

an entrepreneur and the social cost of production.[59] Into the cost account of the private entrepreneur only those items enter for which he has to pay a price, while such items as the maintenance of the unemployed created when he discharges workers, the provision for the victims of occupational diseases and industrial accidents, etc., do not enter, or, as Professor J. M. Clark has shown, are diverted into social overhead costs.[60] On the other side, there are the cases where private producers render services which are not included in the price of the product.

An economic system based on private enterprise can take but very imperfect account of the alternatives sacrificed and realized in production. Most important alternatives, like life, security, and health of the workers, are sacrificed without being accounted for as a cost of production. A socialist economy would be able to put *all* the alternatives into its economic accounting. Thus it would evaluate *all* the services rendered by production and take into the cost accounts *all* the alternatives sacrificed; as a result it would also be able to convert its social overhead costs into prime costs. By doing so it would avoid much of the social waste connected with private enterprise. As Professor Pigou has shown, much of this waste can be removed by proper legislation, taxation, and bounties also within the framework of the present economic system, but a socialist economy can do it with much greater thoroughness.

[59] *The Economics of Welfare,* Pt. II, chap. ix.
[60] J. Maurice Clark, *Studies in the Economics of Overhead Costs* (Chicago, 1923), pp. 25–27, 397–403, 463–64.

A very important case of benefits and costs which the private producer cannot consider arises when external economies or diseconomies of scale are present. In such case the increase in output by one producer increases or diminishes the efficiency of the factors of production engaged by the other producers. Since the social benefit or cost which thus arises is not rewarded to or imposed upon the individual producer, he cannot take it into account in determining his output. And under free competition the number of firms producing a commodity is such that the price of the product is equal to the average cost borne by the private producers. Thus the social benefits and costs due to external economies or diseconomies are not accounted for. In a socialist economy this situation is taken care of automatically by the rule that each industry produce just enough to equalize the *marginal* cost incurred by the industry in producing that amount with the price of the product. External economies and diseconomies arising from a change in the output of the industry appear in the form of a divergence between average and marginal cost incurred by the industry. They are taken care of by the rule to equalize not the average, but the marginal, cost of production with the price of the product.

As a result of the possibility of taking into account *all* the alternatives a socialist economy would not be subject to the fluctuations of the business cycle. Whatever the theoretical explanation of the business cycle, that cumulative shrinkage of demand and output caused by a cumulative reduction of purchasing power could be stopped in a socialist economy. In a socialist economy there can be, of course, grave mistakes and misdirection of investments and production. But such misdirection need not lead to shrinkage of output and unemployment of factors of production spreading over the whole economic system. A private entrepreneur *has* to close his plant when he incurs grave losses. In a socialist economy a mistake is a mistake, too, and has to be corrected. But in making the correction *all* the alternatives gained and sacrificed can be taken into account, and there is no need to correct losses in one part of the economic system by a procedure which creates still further losses by the secondary effect of a cumulative shrinkage of demand and of unemployment of factors of production. Mistakes can be *localized,* a partial overproduction does not need to turn into a general one.[61] Thus the business cycle theorist would lose his subject of study in a socialist economy, but the knowledge accumulated by him would still be useful in finding out ways of preventing mistakes, and methods of correcting those made that would not lead to further losses.

The possibility of determining the distribution of incomes so as to maximize social welfare and of taking *all* the alternatives into the economic account makes a socialist

[61] The decisions of the Central Planning Board being guided, not by the aim to secure a maximum profit on each separate investment, but by considerations of making the best use of all the productive resources available in the whole economic system, an amount of investment sufficient to provide full employment for all factors of production would be always maintained.

economy, from the economist's point of view, superior to a competitive regime with private ownership of the means of production and with private enterprise,[62] but especially superior to a competitive capitalist economy where a large part of the participants in the economic system are deprived of any property of productive resources other than their labor. However, the actual capitalist system is not one of perfect competition; it is one where oligopoly and monopolistic competition prevail. This adds a much more powerful argument to the economist's case for socialism. The wastes of monopolistic competition have received so much attention in recent theoretical literature that there is no need to repeat the argument here. The capitalist system is far removed from the model of a competitive economy as elaborated by economic theory. And even if it conformed to it, it would be, as we have seen, far from maximizing social welfare. Only a socialist economy can fully satisfy the claim made by many economists with regard to the achievements of free competition. The *formal* analogy, however, between the principles of distribution of resources

[62] The deficiencies due to inequality of incomes would be absent in a competitive system where the private ownership of the means of production is equally distributed among the population. (Marx called such a system *einfache Warenproduktion*.) Such a system is incompatible with large-scale industry. But, on account of the approximate equality of incomes in such a system, a socialist economy could partly embody such a system in its own. Therefore, socialism does not need to abolish the private ownership of the means of production in small-scale industry and farming, provided large-scale production is not more economical in these particular fields. By appropriate legislation, taxes, and bounties a socialist economy can induce those small-scale entrepreneurs to take *all* alternatives into consideration and avoid the danger of their causing serious business fluctuations.

in a socialist and in a competitive regime of private enterprise makes the scientific technique of the theory of economic equilibrium which has been worked out for the latter also applicable to the former.

The actual capitalist system is much better described by the analysis of Mrs. Robinson and of Professor Chamberlin than by that of Walras and of Marshall. But the work of the latter two will be more useful in solving the problems of a socialist system. As a result, Professor Chamberlin and Mrs. Robinson face the danger of losing their jobs under socialism, unless they agree to be transferred to the department of economic history to provide students of history with the theoretical apparatus necessary to understand what will appear to a future generation as the craze and folly of a past epoch.

Against these advantages of a socialist economy the economist might put the disadvantage resulting from the arbitrariness of the rate of capital accumulation, if accumulation is performed "corporately." A rate of accumulation which does not reflect the preferences of the consumers as to the time-shape of the flow of income may be regarded as a diminution of social welfare. But it seems that this deficiency may be regarded as overbalanced by the advantages enumerated. Besides, saving is also in the present economic order determined only partly by pure utility considerations, and *the rate of saving is affected much more by the distribution of incomes, which is irrational from the economist's point of view.* Further, as Mr. Robertson has already shown,[63] and Mr. Keynes has elaborated in his analysis of the factors determining the total volume of employment,[64] in a capitalist economy the public's attempt to save may be frustrated by not being followed by an appropriate rate of investment, with the result that poverty instead of increased wealth results from the people's propensity to save. Thus the rate of accumulation determined "corporately" in a socialist society may prove to be, from the economic point of view, much more rational than the actual rate of saving in capitalist society is.

There is also the argument which might be raised against socialism with regard to the efficiency of public officials as compared with private entrepreneurs as managers of production. Strictly speaking, these public officials must be compared with corporation officials under capitalism, and not with private small-scale entrepreneurs. The argument thus loses much of its force. The discussion of this argument belongs to the field of sociology rather than of economic theory and must therefore be dispensed with here. By doing so we do not mean, however, to deny its great importance. It seems to us, indeed, that *the real danger of socialism is that of a bureaucratization of economic life,* and not the impossibility of coping with the problem of allocation of resources. Unfortunately, we do not see how the same, or even greater, danger can be averted under

[63] D. H. Robertson, *Banking Policy and the Price Level* (London, 1926), pp. 45–47; *Money* (rev. ed., London, 1929), pp. 93–97.

[64] J. M. Keynes, *The General Theory of Employment, Interest, and Money* (London, 1936).

monopolistic capitalism. Officials subject to democratic control seem preferable to private corporation executives who practically are responsible to nobody.

However, the really important point in discussing the economic merits of socialism is not that of comparing the equilibrium position of a socialist and of a capitalist economy with respect to social welfare. Interesting as such a comparison is for the economic theorist, it is not the real issue in the discussion of socialism. The real issue is *whether the further maintenance of the capitalist system is compatible with economic progress.*

That capitalism has been the carrier of the greatest economic progress ever witnessed in the history of the human race the socialists are the last to deny. Indeed, there has scarcely ever been a more enthusiastic eulogy of the revolutionizing achievements of the capitalist system than that contained in the Communist Manifesto. The bourgeoisie, states the Manifesto, "has been the first to show what man's activity can bring about. It has accomplished wonders far surpassing Egyptian pyramids, Roman aqueducts, and Gothic cathedrals; it has conducted expeditions that put in the shade all former exoduses of nations and crusades. . . . The bourgeoisie, by the rapid improvement of all instruments of production, by the immensely facilitated means of communication, draws all, even the barbarian, nations into civilization. . . . The bourgeoisie, during its rule of scarce one hundred years, has created more massive and more colossal productive forces than have all preceding generations together. Subjection of Nature's forces to man, machinery, application of chemistry to industry and agriculture, steam navigation, railways, electric telegraphs, clearing of whole continents for cultivation, canalization of rivers, whole populations conjured out of the ground— what earlier century had even a presentiment that such productive forces slumbered in the lap of social labor?" The question arises, however, whether the institutions of private property of the means of production and of private enterprise will continue indefinitely to foster economic progress, or whether, at a certain stage of technical development, they turn from being promoters into becoming shackles of further advance. The last is the contention of the socialists.

The unprecedented economic progress of the last two hundred years is due to innovations increasing the productivity of a given combination of factors of production, or creating new commodities and services. The effects of such innovations on the profits of private enterprise are twofold: (1) The entrepreneur introducing an innovation gains an immediate, though under free competition only temporary, profit or increase in profit. (2) The entrepreneurs using the antiquated means of production, or producing competing goods which are replaced by cheaper rivals, suffer losses which ultimately lead to a devaluation of the capital invested in their business; on the other side there may be entrepreneurs who profit by new demand created in consequence of the innovation. In any case, each innovation is necessarily connected with a loss of value of certain old investments.

In a competitive regime, with the parametric function of prices and with free entry of new firms into each industry, entrepreneurs and investors *have* to submit to the losses and devaluation of old investments resulting from innovations, for there is no possibility of counteracting these innovations. The only way for entrepreneurs to meet the situation is to try to introduce innovations in their own business, which, in turn, inflict losses on others. But when business units become so large as to make the parametric function of prices and the possibility of free entry of new firms (and investments) into the industry ineffective, there arises a tendency to avoid a devaluation of the capital invested. A private enterprise, unless forced by competition to do otherwise, will introduce innovations only when the old capital invested is amortized, or if the reduction of cost is so pronounced as to offset the devaluation of the capital already invested, i.e., if the average total cost becomes lower than the average prime cost of producing with the old machinery or equipment. But such slowing up of technical progress is against the social interest.[65]

The tendency to maintain the value of existing investments becomes even more powerful when the ownership

[65] It is in the interest of society that *any* improvement available be introduced, irrespective of what happens to the value of capital already invested. If the improvement allows the commodity to be produced at an average total cost which is lower than the average prime cost of producing it with the old machinery, a replacement of the old machinery by the new is obviously in the interest of the public. But even if the average total cost of the new method of production is not

of the capital invested is separated from the entrepreneurial function, as is increasingly the case in modern so-called *financial capitalism*. For the industrial enterprise has to replace the full value of the capital invested or fail. This is strictly true if the financing of the enterprise has been made through bond issues, but even if it has been made by stock issues a pronounced decline of stock quotations injures its financial prestige.

But the maintenance of the value of invested capital is not compatible with cost-reducing innovations. This has been pointed out very brilliantly by Professor Robbins:

The maintenance of the value of invested capital may very well mean that producers who find prospects in one industry more attractive than the prospects in any others are prevented from entering it, that cost-reducing improvements of technique which would greatly cheapen the commodity to consumers are held up, that the "wasteful competition" of people who are content to serve the consumer for lower returns than before is prevented from reducing prices. Every schoolboy knows that the cheapness which comes from importing corn is incompatible with the maintenance of the value of the corn lands which would be cultivated if import were restricted. The platitudes of the theory of international trade do not lose any of their force if they are applied to domestic competition. The argument, for instance, that road transport diminishes the value of railway capital has just as much and just as little force as the argument that cheap food lowers the value of agricultural property. . . . Economic progress, in the sense of

---

lower than the average prime cost of producing with the old machinery, its introduction is in the interest of the public. In this case both the old and the new machinery ought to be employed in production, the public getting the benefit of lower prices. The loss of value of the old capital invested is exactly compensated by the public's gain in consequence of price reduction. Cf. Pigou, *The Economics of Welfare*, pp. 190–92.

cheapening of commodities, is not compatible with the preservation of the value already invested in particular industries.[66]

Therefore, when the maintenance of the value of the capital already invested becomes the chief concern of the entrepreneurs, further economic progress has to stop, or, at least, to slow down considerably.

And in present capitalism the maintenance of the value of the particular investment has, indeed, become the chief concern. Accordingly, interventionism and restrictionism are the dominant economic policies.[67] But since innovations very frequently reduce the value of capital in other firms or industries rather than in that which introduces them, innovations cannot be stopped altogether. When the pressure of new innovations becomes so strong as to destroy the artificially preserved value of the old investments a frightful economic collapse is the result. The stability of the capitalist system is shaken by the alternation of attempts to stop economic progress in order to protect old investments and tremendous collapses when those attempts fail. The increasing instability of business conditions can be remedied only by either giving up the attempts to protect the value of old investments or successfully stopping innovations.

But holding back technical progress would involve the capitalist system in a new set of difficulties because there would be no profitable investment opportunities for capi-

---

[66] *The Great Depression*, p. 141.

[67] The protection of monopoly privileges and of particular investments is also the chief source of the imperialist rivalries of the Great Powers.

tal accumulation. Without technical progress (of the labor-saving kind), discovery of new natural resources, or considerable increase in population (and the latter two are not sufficient in our day to outbalance a lack of the first), the marginal *net* productivity of capital is liable to fall to a level insufficient to compensate the liquidity preference of the capital holders. This result is even more accentuated when a part of the industries enjoy a monopoly position which enables them to protect the value of their investments, for the fact that new capital finds free entry only into those industries where free competition still prevails depresses the marginal *net* productivity of capital much more than would otherwise be the case. As substantiated by Mr. Keynes' brilliant analysis,[68] this would lead to a deflationary pressure resulting in chronic unemployment of the factors of production.

To prevent such chronic unemployment the state would have to undertake great public investments, thus replacing the private capitalist where the latter refuses to enter because of the low rate of return on the investment. Unless further capital accumulation is effectively prohibited, the state would have to replace the private capitalists more and

[68] See *The General Theory of Employment*, pp. 217–21 and 308–09. It ought to be mentioned that the difficulties presented to the capitalist system through capital accumulation finding no outlet in profitable investment opportunities were discussed, though no definite conclusions were reached, by a long series of writers of the Marxist school; Tugan-Baranowski, Hilferding, Rosa Luxemburg, Otto Bauer, Bucharin, Sternberg, Grossmann, and Strachey are only the most important of them. These writers have, however, been much more successful in explaining the bearing of those difficulties on the imperialist policy of the capitalist states.

more in their function as investors. Thus the capitalist system seems to face an unescapable dilemma: holding back technical progress leads, through the exhaustion of profitable investment opportunities, to a state of chronic unemployment which can be remedied only by a policy of public investments on an ever-increasing scale, while a continuance of technical progress leads to the instability due to the policy of protecting the value of old investments which has been previously described.

It seems to us that the tendency to maintain the value of old investments can be removed successfully only by the abolition of private enterprise and of the private ownership of capital and natural resources, at least in those industries where such tendency prevails. Two other ways of removing it are conceivable.

One way would be the return to free competition. This way, however, does not seem to be possible because of the large size of modern business units. In a system based on the pursuit of private profit each entrepreneur has the natural tendency to exploit all possibilities of increasing his profit. The tendency to restrict competition is as natural for private enterprise as the tendency to protect the value of old investments is natural for private ownership of capital. As Adam Smith long ago remarked: "The interest of dealers in any particular branch of trade or manufactures is always in some respect different from, or even opposite to, that of the public. To widen the market and to narrow the competition is always the interest of the dealers. To widen the market may frequently be agreeable enough to the interest of the public, but to narrow the competition must be always against it."[69] Or in another passage: "People of the same trade seldom meet together, even for merriment or diversion, but the conversation ends in a conspiracy against the public, or in some contrivance to raise prices."[70] No private entrepreneur or private capitalist can be expected to renounce voluntarily an opportunity to raise his profit or the value of his investment:

> Al mondo non fur mai persone ratte
> a far lor pro ed a fuggir lor danno.
> *(Inferno,* Canto II)

The system of free competition is a rather peculiar one. Its mechanism is one of *fooling* entrepreneurs. It requires the pursuit of maximum profit in order to function, but it destroys profits when they are actually pursued by a larger number of people. However, this game of blindman's buff with the pursuit of maximum profit is possible only as long as the size of the business unit is small and the number of entrepreneurs is consequently large. But with the growth of large-scale industry and the centralization of financial control the pursuit of maximum profit destroys free competition.

The picture would not be complete without adding that political interference in economic life is frequently used to protect profits or investments.[71] This political inter-

---

[69] *Wealth of the Nations* (Cannan's 3d ed., London, 1922), Vol. I, p. 250.
[70] *Ibid.,* p. 130.
[71] Much more frequently in Europe than in the United States.

vention is also a result of the growing size of industrial and financial units. Small-scale enterprises are too small to be politically significant, but the economic power of big corporations and banking interests is too great not to have serious political consequences. As long as the maximization of profit is the basis of all business activities it is unavoidable that industrial and financial corporations should try to use their economic power to increase profits or the value of their investments by proper state intervention.[72] And unless the executive and legislative organs of the state are abstract metaphysical entities beyond the reach of any earthly influence, they will yield to the pressure of those powers. A return to free competition could be accomplished only by splitting up the large-scale business units to destroy their economic and political power. This could be attained only at the cost of giving up large-scale production and the great economic achievements of mass production that are associated with it. Such an artificially maintained system of free competition would have to prohibit the use of advanced technology.

There is a second possible way of overcoming the tend-

[72] This has also an important influence on the selection of business leaders. Under free competition the most successful leader of a business enterprise is he who is able to produce at the lowest cost. With interventionism and restrictionism the best businessman is he who best knows how to influence in his interest the decisions of the organs of the state (in regard to tariffs, government subsidies or orders, advantageous import quotas, etc.). A special ability in this direction may well compensate for the incapacity to produce at a low cost. The best lobbyist becomes the most successful business leader. What formerly was regarded as a special trait of the munitions industry becomes in interventionist capitalism the general rule.

ency to maintain the value of old investments: the control of production and investments by the government with the purpose of preventing monopoly and restrictionism. Such control would signify planning of production and investment without removing private enterprise and private ownership of the means of production. However, such planning can scarcely be successful. The great economic power of corporations and banks being what it is, it would be they who would control the public planning authorities rather than the reverse. The result would be planning for monopoly and restrictionism, the reverse of what was aimed at.

But even if this could be avoided, such control would be unsuccessful. To retain private property and private enterprise and to force them to do things different from those required by the pursuit of maximum profit would involve a terrific amount of regimentation of investment and enterprise. To realize this one has but to consider that government control preventing restrictionist preservation of the value of old investments would have to force producers to act in a way which imposes on them actual losses of capital. This would upset the financial structure of modern capitalist industry. The constant friction between capitalists and entrepreneurs on the one side and the controlling government authorities on the other side would paralyze business. Besides, the corporations and big banks could use their economic power to defy the government authorities (for instance, by closing their plants, withdrawing investments, or other kinds of economic sabotage). As a result the government would have either to yield, and thus give up any effective interference with the pursuit of maximum profit, or transfer the defying corporations and banks into public ownership and management. The latter would lead straight to socialism.

Thus, monopoly, restrictionism, and interventionism can be done away with only together with private enterprise and the private ownership of the means of production, which, from being promoters, have turned into obstacles, of economic progress. This does not imply the necessity, or wisdom, of abolishing private enterprise and private property of the means of production in those fields where real competition still prevails, i.e., in small-scale industry and farming. In these fields private property of the means of production and private enterprise may well continue to have a useful social function by being more efficient than a socialized industry might be. But the most important part of modern economic life is just as far removed from free competition as it is from socialism;[73] it is choked up with restrictionism of all sorts. When this state of things will have become unbearable, when its incompatibility

[73] According to the United States Senate report on *Industrial Prices and Their Relative Inflexibility* (74th Congress, 1st Session, Document No. 13, p. 10), written by Professor G. C. Means, in the United States "more than one-half of all manufacturing activity is carried on by two hundred big corporations, while big corporations dominate the railroad and public utility fields and play an important role in the fields of construction and distribution." See also A. A. Berle and G. C. Means, *The Modern Corporation and Private Property* (New York, 1933), Bk. I, chap. iii, and A. R. Burns, *The Decline of Competition* (New York, 1936).

with economic progress will have become obvious, and when it will be recognized that it is impossible to return to free competition, or to have successful public control of enterprise and of investment without taking them out of private hands, then socialism will remain as the only solution available. Of course, this solution will be opposed by those classes who have a vested interest in the *status quo*. The socialist solution can, therefore, be carried out only after the political power of those classes has been broken.

VI. ON THE POLICY OF TRANSITION

The preceding treatment of the allocation of resources and of pricing in a socialist economy refers to a socialist system already established. The question does not present any special theoretical difficulty if a sector of small-scale private enterprise and private ownership of the means of production is embodied in the socialist economy. However, on grounds which result from our previous discussion of the problem, this sector should satisfy the following three conditions: (1) Free competition must reign in it; (2) the amount of means of production owned by a private producer (or of the capital owned by a private shareholder in socialized industries) must not be so large as to cause a considerable inequality in the distribution of incomes; and (3) the small-scale production must not be, in the long run, more expensive than large-scale production.

But the problem of transition from capitalism to socialism presents some special problems. Most of those problems refer to the economic measures made necessary by the political strategy of carrying through the transformation of the economic and social order. But there are also some problems which are of a purely economic character and which, therefore, deserve the attention of the economist.

The first question is whether the transfer into public property and management of the means of production and enterprises to be socialized should be the first or the last stage of the policy of transition. In our opinion it should be the first stage. The socialist government must start its policy of transition immediately with the *socialization* of the industries and banks in question. This follows from what has been said before on the possibility of successful government control of private enterprise and private investment. If the socialist government attempted to control or supervise them while leaving them in private hands, there would emerge all the difficulties of forcing a private entrepreneur or capitalist to act differently than the pursuit of profit commands. At best the constant friction between the supervising government agencies and the entrepreneurs and capitalists would paralyze business. After such an unsuccessful attempt the socialist government would have either to give up its socialist aims or to proceed to socialization.

The opinion is almost generally accepted that the process of socialization must be as gradual as possible in order to avoid grave economic disturbance. Not only right-wing socialists but also left-wing socialists and communists[74] hold this theory of economic gradualism. While the latter two regard a speedy socialization as necessary on grounds of political strategy, they nevertheless usually admit that, concerning economic considerations alone, a gradual socialization is much the preferable course. Unfortunately, the economist cannot share this theory of economic gradualism.

An economic system based on private enterprise and private property of the means of production can work only as long as the security of private property and of income derived from property and from enterprise is maintained. The very existence of a government bent on introducing socialism is a constant threat to this security. Therefore, the capitalist economy cannot function under a socialist government unless the government is socialist in name only. If the socialist government socializes the coal mines today and declares that the textile industry is going to be socialized after five years, we can be quite certain that the textile industry will be ruined before it will be socialized. For the owners threatened with expropriation have no inducement to make the necessary investments and improvements and to manage them efficiently. And no government supervision or administrative measures can cope effectively with the passive resistance and sabotage of the ·owners and

[74] How far the Russian Bolsheviks, before taking power, conceived socialization as a gradual process can be seen from Lenin's "The Threatening Catastrophe and How to Fight It," *Collected Works,* Vol. XXI, Bk. I (International Publishers, New York, 1932).

managers. There may be exceptions in the case of industries managed by technicians rather than by businessmen. Those technicians, if assured that they would keep their places, might be quite sympathetic to the idea of transfer of the industry into public ownership. Also a scheme of proper compensation for expropriated owners might help to solve the difficulty. But to be fully effective the compensation would have to be so high as to cover the full value of the objects expropriated. The capital value of these objects having been maintained on an artificially high level by monopolistic and restrictionist practices, the compensation would have to be far in excess of the value of these objects in a socialist economy (and also under free competition in capitalism). This would impose on the socialist government a financial burden which would make any further advance in the socialization program almost impossible. Therefore, a program of comprehensive socialization can scarcely be achieved by gradual steps.

A socialist government really intent upon socialism has to decide to carry out its socialization program at one stroke, or to give it up altogether.[75] The very coming into power of such a government must cause a financial panic and economic collapse. Therefore, the socialist government must either guarantee the immunity of private property

[75] This is true of any policy aiming at a radical change in property relations, not only of socialization. For instance, an agrarian revolution like that taking place in Spain and due in many countries of eastern Central Europe cannot proceed gradually if agricultural production is not to be ruined by many years of uncertainty.

and private enterprise in order to enable the capitalist economy to function normally, in doing which it gives up its socialist aims, or it must go through resolutely with its socialization program at maximum speed.[76] Any hesitation, any vacillation and indecision would provoke the inevitable economic catastrophe.[77] Socialism is not an economic policy for the timid.

On the other hand, as a complement to its resolute policy of speedy socialization, the socialist government has to declare in an unmistakable way that all property and enterprise not explicitly included in the socialization measures is going to remain in private hands, and to *guarantee its absolute security*. It has to make it absolutely clear to everybody that socialism is not directed against private property as such, but only against that special type of private property which creates social privileges to the detriment of the great majority of the people or creates obstacles to economic progress, and that, consequently, all private property of the means of production and all private enterprise which have a useful social function will enjoy the full protection and support of the socialist state. To avoid

[76] In the necessity of choosing between these two alternatives lies the tragedy of all right-wing socialist governments.

[77] This was brought out clearly by the experience of the first eight months of Bolshevist power in Russia. The Soviet government tried honestly to avoid speedy and wholesale socialization of industries. An economic collapse was the result. Most of the socialization decrees during those months were emergency measures which had to be taken because the old owners were unable to run their factories without the necessary security of property and profit and without the necessary authority over the workers. For details see Dobb, *Russian Economic Development since the Revolution* (New York, 1928), chap. ii.

the growth of an atmosphere of panic in this sector of private property and private enterprise the socialist government may have to prove the seriousness of its intentions by some *immediate deeds in favor of the small entrepreneurs and small property holders* (including holders of saving deposits and small stock and bondholders).

To be successful, the socialist government must put itself at the head of a great mass movement against monopoly and restrictionism, against imperialism and the concentration of economic control by a few, against social and economic instability and insecurity. Only under the impetus of such a mass movement, embracing the majority of the population, will it be able to carry out speedily a bold program of socialization. In the absence of such a mass movement, there is little a socialist government in office can achieve. For, as we have seen, if socialization cannot be achieved by a great and bold stroke, the government has to give up its socialist aims altogether.

If it gives up these aims it remains socialist in name only, its real function being the administration of the capitalist economy, which can be carried on successfully only if the property of the capitalists and the freedom of the capitalist entrepreneurs to realize their profits are safeguarded. In such a case the socialists would do much better to turn over the office to a capitalist government, which, having the confidence of the business world, is more fit to administer a capitalist society.

There exist, however, special situations where a socialist

government, even if it has not the power to achieve a comprehensive socialization, may have a useful task to fulfill, a task which a capitalist government may be unable to carry out. If the marginal efficiency of capital (as defined by Mr. Keynes[78]) is very low and the liquidity preference of the capitalists is very high, as is usually the case in a depression, a bold program of public investments is needed to restore employment to a higher level. In principle, there is no reason why a capitalist government should not be able to perform those investments. But since they have to be effected without regard to the low rate of return upon them, i.e., in violation of the fundamental principle of the capitalist economy that investments ought to be made for profit only, they may appear to all the capitalist parties as "unsound." Thus it may take a socialist government, free from the ballast of bourgeois prejudices about economic policies,[79] to restore the capitalist economy. In such circumstances the socialists might form a government with a "labor plan" to attack unemployment and the depression. If the labor plan is carried out successfully the popularity of the socialists will be greatly increased.

As the decay of capitalism continues, there will arise

[78] *The General Theory of Employment,* chap. ii.

[79] It ought to be mentioned, however, that socialist governments have sometimes proved to be much more affected by the bourgeois prejudices regarding economic and financial policies than capitalist governments. The reason for it was that by the "soundness" of their policies they wanted to make up for the lack of confidence of the business and financial world. It need nqt be said that even at this price a socialist government scarcely wins the sympathy of the big capitalist and financial interests while it forfeits its only chance of success in its economic policies.

many occasions when the capitalist parties will prove unable to enact reforms which are necessary even from the point of view of securing normal functioning of the capitalist society. Being sociologically closely connected with the dominating vested interests, viz., monopoly and financial interests, the capitalist parties may be utterly incapable of any action that injures the vested interests with which they are associated, even if these interests should prevent the normal functioning of the capitalist economy as a whole. And the greater the economic and political instability of the capitalist system, the more nervous the capitalist parties may become about changes, fearing that to admit the necessity of changes will open the road to socialism. Thus the capitalist parties may become reluctant to carry out even those adjustments and reforms that have become necessary within the framework of the capitalist order. In such cases, *if a great popular demand* for such reforms arises, the socialists may have to come to the public with a labor plan to carry out the reforms demanded and form a government pledged to put the plan into action.[80] If they do this successfully their position will be strengthened. Thus a labor plan, or a series of labor plans, may prove an important link in the evolution which finally must issue in the emergence of an anti-capitalist mass

[80] The possibility of such a policy presupposes, of course, the existence of democratic political institutions. Should, however, the threatened capitalist vested interests attempt to make this work of the socialists impossible by trying to overthrow the institutions of political democracy, a social revolution would result automatically from the very necessity of taking the economic power out of the hands of the enemies of democracy.

movement of irresistible power and impetus enforcing a wholesale reconstruction of the economic and social order.

But even a socialist government whose purposes are confined within the limits of such a labor plan needs boldness and decision in carrying out its program; otherwise it degenerates into a mere administrator of the existing capitalist society.

Marshall placed caution among the chief qualities an economist should have. Speaking of the rights of property he observed: "It is the part of responsible men to proceed cautiously and tentatively in abrogating or modifying even such rights as may seem to be inappropriate to the ideal conditions of social life."[81] But he did not fail to indicate that the great founders of modern economics were strong not only in caution but also in courage.[82] Caution was the great virtue of the nineteenth-century economist who was concerned with minor improvements in the existing economic system. The delicate mechanism of supply and demand might be damaged and the initiative and efficiency of businessmen might be undermined by an improvident step. But the economist who is called upon to advise a socialist government faces a different task, and the qualities needed for this task are different, too. For there exists only one economic policy which he can commend to a socialist government as likely to lead to success. This is a policy of *revolutionary courage*.

[81] *Principles of Economics*, p. 48.
[82] *Ibid.*, p. 47.

Appendix

THE ALLOCATION OF RESOURCES UNDER SOCIALISM
IN MARXIST LITERATURE

It is interesting to see how the problem of allocation of resources in a socialist economy is solved by the leading writers of the socialist movement and to compare their solution with that offered by modern economic theory. As the theoretical foundations of the socialist movement have been elaborated chiefly by the Marxists, it is their views which are of foremost interest. For this purpose let us review briefly the statements of some of the most prominent of them.

To begin with Marx, it is not difficult to prove by quotations that he was well aware of the problem, though he tried to solve it in a rather unsatisfactory way. Discussing the economics of Robinson Crusoe in *Das Kapital,* he writes:

Moderate though he be, yet some few wants he has to satisfy, and must therefore do a little useful work of various sorts. . . . Necessity itself compels him to apportion his time accurately between his different kinds of work. . . . This our friend Robinson soon learns by experience, and having rescued a watch, ledger, and pen and ink from the wreck, commences, like a true-born Briton, to keep a set of books. His stock book contains a list of the objects of utility that belong to him, of the operations necessary for their production, and, lastly, of the labor-time that definite quantities of those objects have, on the average, cost him. All the relations between Robinson and the objects that form this wealth of his own creation are here so simple and clear as to be intelligible without exertion even to Mr. Sedley Taylor. And yet those relations contain all that is essential to the determination of value.[83]

And he continues:

Let us now picture to ourselves, by way of change, a community of free individuals, carrying on their work with the means of production in common. . . . All the characteristics of Robinson's labor are here repeated, but with this difference, that they are social instead of individual. . . . The total product of our community is a social product. One portion serves as fresh means of production and remains social. But another portion is consumed by the members as means of subsistence. The mode of this distribution will vary with the productive organization of the community, and the degree of historical development attained by the producers. We will assume, but merely for the sake of a parallel with the production of commodities, that the share of each producer in the means of subsistence is determined by his labor-time. Labor-time would, in that case, play a double part. Its apportionment in accordance with a definite social plan maintains the proper proportion between the different kinds of work to be done and the various wants of the community. On the other hand, it also serves as a measure of the portion of common labor borne by each individual and of his share in the part of the total product destined for individual consumption.[84]

Each worker would enjoy freedom of choice in consumption within the limits thus determined: "He receives from society a voucher that he has contributed such and such a quantity of labor (after deduction from his labor for the common fund) and draws through this voucher on

[83] *Capital* (E. Untermann, trans., C. H. Kerr, Chicago, 1906), Vol. I, p. 88 (p. 43 of 6th German ed., Meissner, Hamburg, 1909).
[84] *Ibid.*, pp. 90–91 (p. 45 of 6th German ed.).

the social storehouse as much of the means of consumption as costs the same quantity of labor."[85]

The importance of the problem of allocating resources is stated very clearly in a letter written in 1868 to Kugelmann:

Every child knows that a country which ceased to work, I will not say for a year, but for a few weeks, would die. Every child knows, too, that the mass of products corresponding to the different needs require different and quantitatively determined masses of the total labor of society. That this necessity of distributing social labor in definite proportions cannot be done away with by the *particular form* of social production, but can only change the *form it assumes,* is self-evident. No natural laws can be done away with. What can change, in changing historical circumstances, is the *form* in which these laws operate. And the form in which this particular division of labor operates, in a state of society where the inter-connection of social labor is manifested in the *private exchange* of the individual products of labor, is precisely the *exchange value* of these products.[86]

The passages quoted show that Marx was fully aware of the problem of allocation of resources in a socialist economy. However, he seems to have thought of labor as the only kind of scarce resource to be distributed between different uses and wanted to solve the problem by the labor

---

[85] *Critique of the Gotha Programme* (London, 1933), p. 29. Inaccuracies in the translation have been corrected by the author.

[86] *The Correspondence of Marx and Engels* (International Publishers, New York, 1934), p. 246. This and some other statements disprove the generally accepted view that Marx regarded *all* economic laws as being of an historico-relative character. His position seems to have been, however, that the economic laws of universal validity are so self-evident that there is scarcely need for a special scientific technique for their study, and economic science ought to concentrate, therefore, upon investigating the particular form these laws assume in a definite institutional framework. Cf. Engels, *Anti-Dühring* (12th ed., Berlin, 1923), pp. 149–50.

theory of value. The unsatisfactory character of this solution need not be argued here, after all our preceding discussion of the subject. Professor Pierson and Professor Mises have certainly merited the gratitude of the student of the problem by exposing the inadequacy of this simplicist solution.[87]

But even accepting the labor theory of value as a basis for the solution of the problem, the question of utility (or of demand) cannot be avoided, or the amounts of the various goods to be produced would be indeterminate. This was recognized clearly by Engels: "The utility yielded by the various consumption goods, weighted against each other and against the amount of labor required to produce them, will ultimately determine the plan."[88] Whoever knows the role the concept of *gesellschaftliches Beduerfnis* plays in the third volume of *Das Kapital* has to admit that Marx was well aware of the role demand (or utility) has

[87] N. G. Pierson, "The Problem of Value in the Socialist Society," reprinted in *Collectivist Economic Planning*, pp. 76ff.; von Mises, "Economic Calculation in the Socialist Commonwealth," *ibid.*, pp. 113ff.

[88] *Anti-Dühring*, pp. 335–36. With some benevolent interpretation this statement of Engels may be regarded, indeed, as containing all the essentials of the modern solution. Interpreting the amount of labor necessary to produce a certain good as the *marginal* amount, all costs may be reduced, in long-period equilibrium, to labor-costs. The prices of the services of natural resources may be regarded as differential rents, and if capital accumulation has been carried on as far as to reduce the marginal *net* productivity of capital to zero, as a socialist society would tend to do (see page 85 above), interest charges are eliminated. Thus the production of each commodity has to be carried so far as to make the ratio of the marginal amount of labor used in producing the different commodities equal to the ratio of the marginal utilities (and of the prices) of those commodities. But such long-period solution eliminating interest would be of little use for practical purposes.

in determining the allocation of resources, though, not unlike Ricardo,[89] he was unable to find a clear functional expression of the law of demand. The limitations of Marx and Engels are those of the classical economists.

From Marx and Engels let us pass to Kautsky, who more than anybody else has contributed to the propagation of Marxian ideas the world over. In a lecture given in 1902 entitled "The Day after the Revolution,"[90] which to a certain extent was an answer to Professor Pierson's challenge, Kautsky formulates his view as to the role of money and prices in a socialist economy. He makes it quite clear that, as a result of freedom of choice in consumption and of freedom of choice of occupation, money and prices have to exist also in a socialist economy. He writes thus:

Money is the simplest means known up to the present time which makes it possible in as complicated a mechanism as that of the modern productive process, with its tremendous far-reaching division of labor, to secure the circulation of products and their distribution to the individual members of society. It is the means which make it possible for each one to satisfy his necessities according to his individual inclination (to be sure within the bounds of his economic power).[91]

And with regard to the allocation of labor to the different industries in a socialist economy he observes:

. . . since the laborers cannot be assigned by military discipline and against their wishes to the various branches of industry, so it may happen that too many laborers rush into certain branches of

[89] Cf. Ricardo's treatment of demand in connection with the theory of rent.
[90] Published as a second part of *The Social Revolution*. Passages here quoted follow the edition by Kerr, Chicago, 1907.
[91] *Ibid.*, p. 129.

industry while a lack of laborers is the rule in the others. The necessary balance can then only be brought about by the reduction of wages where there are too many laborers and the raising of them in those branches of industry where there is a lack of laborers until the point is reached where every branch has as many laborers as it can use.[92]

Unfortunately, Kautsky did not enter into the question of the criteria to be used in planning production. However, he carried his ideas further in his book *The Labour Revolution,* written in 1922.[93] Raising again the point that socialism does not imply the abolition of money, he states very clearly the connection of the problem with the freedom of choice in consumption:

Without money only two kinds of economy are possible: First of all the primitive economy already mentioned. Adapted to modern dimensions, this would mean that the whole of productive activity in the State would form a single factory, under one central control, which would assign its task to each single business, collect all the products of the entire population, and assign to each business its means of production and to each consumer his means of consumption in kind. The ideal of such a condition is the prison or the barracks. This barbarous monotony lurks in fact behind the ideas of the "natural economy" of Socialism.[94]

Quoting a socialist enthusiast of "natural economy" who finds no difficulty in rationing consumption, Kautsky remarks:

Assuredly not, if the entire life of a civilized man is to be reduced to war rations, and everybody to have the same quantity of bread,

[92]*Ibid.,* pp. 134–35.
[93]New York, 1925. The title of the German original, published in Berlin in 1922, is *Die proletarische Revolution und ihr Programm.*
[94]*The Labour Revolution.* p. 260.

meat, accommodation, clothes, personal taste not playing any part and distinctions not being observed, although there is to be special cooking for poets and children. Unfortunately, we are not told how many hundredweights of books are to be allotted to each citizen in the course of a year, and how frequently the inhabitants of each house are to go to the cinematograph.[95]

The other kind of socialist economy which might do without money is, according to Kautsky, that in which all commodities would be free goods.[96]

Kautsky also recognizes the necessity of a price system for cost accounting. Like all Marxists of the old school he uses the labor theory of value as a basis for elucidating the problem of the distribution of resources in a socialist economy. But what is most important, he quite explicitly admits the practical impossibility of calculating the amount of labor socially necessary to produce a given commodity: "Consider what colossal labor would be involved in calculating for each product the amount of labor it had cost from its initial to its final stage, including transport and other incidental labor."[97] Hence the necessity of a price system: "The appraisement of commodities according to the labor contained in them, which could not be achieved by the most complicated State machine imaginable, we find to be an accomplished fact in the shape of the transmitted prices, as the result of a long historical process, imperfect and inexact, but nevertheless the only practical foundation for the smooth functioning of the economic process of circulation."[98] Thus money prices are the basis of economic

[95] Ibid.   [96] Ibid., p. 261.   [97] Ibid., p. 264.   [98] Ibid., p. 267.

accounting: "Whatever may be the lines upon which a socialist society is organized, very careful accountancy would be required. . . . This object would be quite impossible of attainment if the incomings and outcomings were entered *in kind*."[99]

The great leader of orthodox Marxism in pre-war times knows, of course, very well the distinction between the Marxian concept of capitalism and that of a money economy:

Thousands of years passed before a capitalist mode of production came into existence. As the measure of value and means of circulation of products money will continue to exist in a socialist society until the dawn of that blessed second phase of communism which we do not yet know whether will ever be more than a pious wish, similar to the Millennial Kingdom.[1]

Finally, he concludes:

The monetary system is a machine which is indispensable for the function of a society with a widely ramified division of labor. . . . It would be a relapse into barbarism to destroy this machine, in order to resort to the primitive expedients of natural economy. This method of combating capitalism recalls the simple workers of the first decades of the last century who thought they would make an end to capitalist exploitation if they smashed the machines which they found to hand. It is not our desire to destroy the machines, but to render them serviceable to society, so that they may be shaped into a means of the emancipation of labor.[2]

But are perhaps these views of Kautsky's a heretical deviation from the orthodox line of Marxist thought?

[99] *Ibid.*, p. 262.
[1] *Ibid.*
[2] *Ibid.*, p. 270.

Maybe they are not representative of modern Marxists, a large part of whom are bitter opponents of the political strategy advocated by him. Let us examine the views of another group of Marxist leaders, the following quotation from Trotsky to begin with:

If there existed the universal mind that projected itself into the scientific fancy of Laplace . . . such a mind could, of course, draw up *a priori* a faultless and an exhaustive economic plan, beginning with the number of hectares of wheat and down to the last button for a vest. In truth, the bureaucracy often conceives that just such a mind is at its disposal; that is why it so easily frees itself from the control of the market and of Soviet democracy. But in reality the bureaucracy errs frightfully in this appraisal of its spiritual resources. . . . The innumerable living participants of economy, State as well as private, collective as well as individual, must give notice of their needs and of their relative strength not only through the statistical determination of plan commissions but by the direct pressure of supply and demand. The plan is checked and to a considerable measure realized through the market. The regulation of the market itself must depend upon the tendencies that are brought out through its medium. The blueprints brought out by the offices must demonstrate their economic expediency through commercial calculation.[3]

And after the critic of the Soviet economic policy let us listen to its leader. In discussing the problem of Soviet trade, Stalin observes:

Then we have to overcome prejudices of another kind. I refer to the Leftist chatter . . . about Soviet trade being a superseded stage. . . . These people, who are as far removed from Marxism as heaven is from earth, evidently do not realize that we shall have

[3] *Soviet Economy in Danger* (Pioneer Publishers, New York, 1932), pp. 29–30.

money for a long time to come, until the first stage of communism, i.e., the socialist stage of development, has been completed.[4]

But Marx anticipated also a second phase of communism (which sometimes is also called communism *sensu stricto* while the first phase is called socialism) in which the distribution of incomes is quite divorced from the labor services performed by the individual and is based on the principle "from each according to his capacity, to each according to his need."[5] Bertrand Russell calls this form of distribution very aptly "free sharing."[6] Free sharing presupposes, of course, that the commodities in question are practically free goods. An outstanding Marxist like Kautsky speaks, therefore, with irony of "that blessed second phase of communism which we do not yet know whether will ever be more than a pious wish, similar to the Millennial Kingdom," while Lenin,[7] Trotsky, and Stalin believe seriously in the possibility of such a stage of economic evolution in the future.

The idea of distributing goods and services by free sharing sounds utopian, indeed. However, if applied to only a part of commodities free sharing is by no means such economic nonsense as might appear at a first glance. The demand for many commodities becomes, from a cer-

[4] Report on the work of the Central Committee of the Communist Party of the Soviet Union made to the Seventeenth Party Congress held in Moscow, January 26 to February 10, 1937.

[5] *Critique of the Gotha Programme*, p. 31.

[6] *Roads to Freedom* (London, 1919), pp. 107ff.

[7] See Lenin, "The State and Revolution," chap. v, sec. 4, *Collected Works*, Vol. XXI, Bk. II (1932); and Trotsky, *The Revolution Betrayed* (New York, 1937), pp. 45–60.

tain point on, quite inelastic. If the price of such a commodity is below, and the consumer's income is above, a certain minimum, the commodity is treated by the consumer *as if it were a free good*. The commodity is consumed in such quantity that the want it serves to satisfy is perfectly *saturated*. Take, for instance, salt. Well-to-do people do the same with bread or with heating in winter. They do not stop eating bread at a point where the marginal utility of a slice is equal to the marginal utility of its price, nor do they turn down the heat by virtue of a similar consideration. Or would a decline of the price of soap to zero induce them to be so much more liberal in its use? Even if the price were zero, the amount of salt, bread, fuel, and soap consumed by well-to-do people would not increase noticeably. With such commodities saturation is reached even at a positive price. If the price is already so low, and incomes so high, that the quantity consumed of those commodities is equal to the *saturation* amount, free sharing can be used as a method of distribution.[8] Certain services are distributed in this way already in our present society.

If a part of the commodities and services is distributed by free sharing, the price system needs to be confined only to the rest of them. However, though the demand for the commodities distributed by free sharing is, within limits, a fixed quantity, a cost has to be accounted for in order to be able to find out the best combination of factors and the

[8] See Russell, *Roads to Freedom*, pp. 109–10.

optimum scale of output in producing them. The money income of the consumers must be reduced by an equivalent of the cost of production of these commodities. This means simply that free sharing provides, so to speak, a "socialized sector" of consumption the cost of which is met by taxation (for the reduction of consumers' money incomes which has just been mentioned is exactly the taxation to cover the consumption by free sharing). Such a sector exists also in capitalist society, comprising, for instance, free education, free medical service by social insurance, public parks, and all the collective wants in Cassel's sense (e.g., street lighting). It is quite conceivable that as wealth increases this sector increases, too, and an increasing number of commodities are distributed by free sharing until, finally, all the prime necessaries of life are provided for in this way, the distribution by the price system being confined to better qualities and luxuries. Thus Marx's second phase of communism may be gradually approached.

The statements quoted are sufficient to prove that the leading writers of the Marxist school were and are quite aware of the necessity of the price system in a socialist economy. It is, therefore, very much exaggerated to say that the Marxian socialists did not see the problem and offered no solution. The truth is that they saw and solved the problem only within the limits of the labor theory of value, being thus subject to all the limitations of the classical theory. But it ought to be mentioned that in Italy, due to the influence of Pareto, the socialist writers were much more advanced in this field. The difference between the traditional Marxist and the modern position on the problem is thus but a difference as to the technique applied. Only the technique provided by the modern method of marginal analysis enables us to solve the problem satisfactorily. Professor Mises' challenge has had the great merit of inducing the socialists to look for a more satisfactory solution of the problem, and it is only too true that many of them became aware of its very existence only after this challenge. But, as we have seen, those of the socialists who did not or do not realize the necessity and importance of an adequate price system and economic accountancy in the socialist economy are backward not only with regard to the present state of economic analysis; they do not even reach up to the great heritage of Marxian doctrine.

Selected Bibliography of Literature on the Theory of Allocation of Resources under Socialism

BARONE, ENRICO, "The Ministry of Production in the Collectivist State," reprinted in *Collectivist Economic Planning* (F. A. von Hayek, ed., Routledge, London, 1935).

DICKINSON, H. D., "Price Formation in a Socialist Community," *Economic Journal*, Vol. XLIII (June, 1933).

DOBB, M. H., "Economic Theory and the Problem of a Socialist Economy," *Economic Journal*, Vol. XLIII (December, 1933).

——, *Political Economy and Capitalism* (London, 1937).

DURBIN, E. F. M., "Economic Calculus in a Planned Economy," *Economic Journal*, Vol. XLVI (December, 1936).

HALL, R. L., *The Economic System in a Socialist State* (London, 1937).

HALM, GEORG, "Further Considerations on the Possibility of Adequate Calculation in a Socialist Community," in *Collectivist Economic Planning* (F. A. von Hayek, ed., Routledge, London, 1935).

HAYEK, F. A. VON, "The Nature and History of the Problem," chap. i; "The Present State of the Debate," chap. v, in *Collectivist Economic Planning* (Routledge, London, 1935).

HEIMANN, EDUARD, *Sozialistische Wirtschafts- und Arbeitsordnung* (Potsdam, 1932).

———, "Planning and the Market System," *Social Research*, Vol. I (November, 1934).

KNIGHT, F. H., "The Place of Marginal Economics in a Collectivist System," *American Economic Review*, supplement to Vol. XXVI (March, 1936).

LANDAUER, CARL, *Planwirtschaft und Verkehrswirtschaft* (Munich, 1931).

———, "Value Theory and Economic Planning," *Plan Age*, Vol. III (October, 1937).

LERNER, A. P., "Economic Theory and Socialist Economy," *Review of Economic Studies*, Vol. II (October, 1934).

———, "A Note on Socialist Economics," *Review of Economic Studies*, Vol. IV (October, 1936).

———, "Statics and Dynamics in Socialist Economics," *Economic Journal*, Vol. XLVII (June, 1937).

MEYER, GERHARD, "A Contribution to the Theory of Socialist Planning," *Plan Age*, Vol. III (October, 1937).

MISES, LUDWIG VON, "Economic Calculation in the Socialist Commonwealth," reprinted in *Collectivist Economic Planning* (F. A. von Hayek, ed., Routledge, London, 1935).

———, *Socialism* (New York, 1937). Translated by J. Kahane from the revised 1932 edition of *Die Gemeinwirtschaft*.

MOSSÉ, ROBERT, "The Theory of Planned Economy: A Study of Some Recent Works," *International Labour Review*, September, 1937. Also reprinted, in slightly shortened form, in *Plan Age*, Vol. III (October, 1937).

PIERSON, N. G., "The Problem of Value in the Socialist Society," reprinted in *Collectivist Economic Planning* (F. A. von Hayek, ed., Routledge, London, 1935).

PIGOU, A. C., *Socialism versus Capitalism* (Macmillan, London, 1937).

ROBBINS, LIONEL, *The Great Depression* (London, 1934).

ROPER, W. CROSBY, *The Problem of Pricing in a Socialist State* (Cambridge, Massachusetts, 1929).

SWEEZY, A. R., "The Economist's Place under Socialism," in *Explorations in Economics: Essays in Honor of F. W. Taussig* (Cambridge, Massachusetts, 1937).

TAYLOR, FRED M., "The Guidance of Production in a Socialist State," *American Economic Review*, Vol. XIX (March, 1929).

WOOTTON, BARBARA, *Plan or No Plan* (London, 1934).

ZASSENHAUS, H., "Ueber die ökonomische Theorie der Planwirtschaft," *Zeitschrift für Nationalökonomie*, Bd. V (September, 1934).

If you're interested . . . . this Paperback . . . . . .
book . . . .
and . . . .
retail . . . .
for . . . .
390 West . . . . Street
New York 10036

McGRAW-HILL PAPERBACKS OF OUTSTANDING INTEREST

Gunnar Myrdal

AN AMERICAN DILEMMA

with a new Preface by the author and a review of recent events by Arnold Rose

Two volumes

Gunnar Myrdal, who has a brilliant international reputation as a social economist, is currently a professor of international economy at the University of Stockholm. Formerly executive secretary of the United Nations Economic Committee for Europe and minister of commerce in the Swedish cabinet, Dr. Myrdal is the author of more than a dozen volumes on economic subjects, including **An International Economy** (1956), **Beyond the Welfare State** (1960), and **Challenge to Affluence** (1963). Although **An American Dilemma** originally appeared in two volumes, this edition reproduces the one-volume Twentieth Anniversary Edition, published by Harper and Row in board binding at $16.50 in 1962. Vol. 1, The Negro in a White Nation, contains Parts I through V of the one-volume edition, as well as the new Preface by the author, and the review of recent events by Arnold Rose. Vol. 2, The Negro Social Structure, contains Parts VI through XI, the Appendixes, and the Index for both volumes.

McGRAW-HILL PAPERBACKS OF OUTSTANDING INTEREST

Joseph A. Schumpeter

BUSINESS CYCLES

A Theoretical, Historical
and Statistical Analysis
of the Capitalist Process

Abridged, with an introduction,
by Rendig Fels

Of his abridgement, Professor Fels writes
"...my first concern has been to preserve
a complete statement of the theory...
my second concern was to retain a full account
of the interpretation of the cyclical history of
one country, in preference to partial accounts
of the three countries that Schumpeter
discussed at length.... [These decisions]
dictated omitting virtually all the statistical
analysis.... I have generally resisted the
temptation to substitute a word or two of my
own, even where doing so could have
saved a good deal of space, on grounds
that my words would have to be in square
brackets which would distract the reader;
but I have, on rare occasions, taken the
liberty of rearranging Schumpeter's
own words."
This abridgement has been reviewed
and approved by the Schumpeter Committee
of Harvard University.

McGRAW-HILL PAPERBACKS
ECONOMICS

Alvin H. Hansen
A GUIDE TO KEYNES
A study of the theories of Keynes, whose ideas have profoundly influenced economic activity in the West. 26046

Alvin H. Hansen
THE AMERICAN ECONOMY
The diversified American economic system and its complex interactions. 26069

Alvin H. Hansen
ECONOMIC ISSUES OF THE 1960s
An original, illuminating discussion of current economic problems. 26073

Alvin H. Hansen
MONETARY THEORY AND FISCAL POLICY
Deals with trends and developments in money supply, national income, public debt management, fiscal policy and the banking system. 26041

Edgar M. Hoover
THE LOCATION OF ECONOMIC ACTIVITY
Discusses the economics of industry location, land utilization, urban structure, and regional development. It is primarily analytical rather than descriptive. 30306

Abba P. Lerner
ECONOMICS OF EMPLOYMENT
In non-technical language the manner by which the level of employment is determined in a modern society, based on Keynesian economics. 37207

R. L. Smyth, Editor
ESSAYS IN ECONOMIC METHOD
Papers presented to the British Association for the Advancement of Science by Jevons, Senior, and others. 59341

George Katona
PSYCHOLOGICAL ANALYSIS OF ECONOMIC BEHAVIOR
An exciting and informative analysis of fluctuations in business cycles, economic eccentricities and the stock market from a psychological point of view. 33376

Joseph W. McGuire
BUSINESS AND SOCIETY
A Paperback Original—the role of business as one of several fundamental centers in our pluralistic society. 45097

Dan T. Smith
FEDERAL TAX REFORM
With a special section prepared for the McGraw-Hill Paperback edition on recent Kennedy administration proposals. 58516

McGRAW-HILL PAPERBACKS
POLITICAL SCIENCE, SOCIOLOGY

H. G. Barnett
INNOVATION: THE BASIS OF CULTURAL CHANGE
A remarkable analysis of creativity in society based on the study of six contrasting cultures. 03793

Theodore Caplow
THE SOCIOLOGY OF WORK
Study of occupational sociology for psychologists, personnel and guidance workers, wage economists and laymen. 09778

Milton Gordon
SOCIAL CLASS IN AMERICAN SOCIOLOGY
The literature of social class is explored in a major study of this significant area of social thought. 23786

Karl Marx
SELECTED WRITINGS IN SOCIOLOGY AND SOCIAL PHILOSOPHY
Edited and translated by T. B. Bottomore and M. Rubel. Illustrates Marx's principal themes, and reveals a society of science which strikingly anticipates modern sociology. 40672

Samuel Ramos
PROFILE OF MAN AND CULTURE IN MEXICO
The first English translation of a true classic by a Mexican scholar who seeks in the culture and psychology of his people a foundation for national growth. 51167

Gaetano Mosca
THE RULING CLASS
A basic work in political science, holding that in every country power is wielded by a relatively small group. Edited and translated by A. Livingston. 43481

William Ebenstein
POLITICAL THOUGHT IN PERSPECTIVE
The great political theorists comment on the ideas of their predecessors in a unique and lively selection for the student and general reader. 18856

Don M. Wolfe
THE IMAGE OF MAN IN AMERICA
Is man's nature predetermined or infinitely plastic? Between these extremes, American intellectual leaders from Jefferson and Horace Mann to Dewey and Kinsey have ranged themselves—with important results for us all. 71350

Ashley Montagu
ANTHROPOLOGY AND HUMAN NATURE
Practical uses of this justifiably popular field as set forth by one of its most eminent practitioners. 42840

Leslie A. White
THE EVOLUTION OF CULTURE
An outstanding work illuminating the development of civilization. 69682

Catalog

If you are interested in a list of fine Paperback
books, covering a wide range of subjects
and interests, send your name and address,
requesting your free catalog, to:

McGraw-Hill Paperbacks
330 West 42nd Street
New York, New York 10036